Mrs. Fixit ™
Pantry Power

by Terri McGraw

MEREDITH₀ BOOKS

Mrs. Fixit ~ Pantry Power

Writer: Terri McGraw
Editor: Paula Marshall
Project Manager: Cathy Long
Contributing Editors: Colleen Rosenthal, Diane Witosky
Graphic Designer: Matthew Eberhart
Copy Chief: Terri Fredrickson
Publishing Operations Manager: Karen Schirm
Edit and Design Production Coordinator: Mary Lee Gavin
Editorial Assistants: Kaye Chabot, Kairee Mullen
Marketing Product Managers: Aparna Pande, Isaac Petersen,
   Gina Rickert, Stephen Rogers, Brent Wiersma, Tyler Woods
Book Production Managers: Pam Kvitne, Marjorie J. Schenkelberg, Rick von Holdt, Mark Weaver
Contributing Copy Editor: Amanda Knief
Contributing Proofreaders: Pam Elizian, Sara Henderson, Ann Marie Sapienza
Contributing Illustrator: Steve Vandervate
Cover Photo: Michael Davis
Indexer: Kathleen Poole

Meredith® Books

Executive Director, Editorial: Gregory H. Kayko
Executive Director, Design: Matt Strelecki
Executive Editor/Group Manager: Denise Caringer

Publisher and Editor in Chief: James D. Blume
Editorial Director: Linda Raglan Cunningham
Executive Director, Marketing: Jeffrey B. Myers
Executive Director, New Business Development: Todd M. Davis
Executive Director, Sales: Ken Zagor
Director, Operations: George A. Susral
Director, Production: Douglas M. Johnston
Business Director: Jim Leonard

Vice President and General Manager: Douglas J. Guendel

Meredith Publishing Group

President: Jack Griffin
Senior Vice President: Bob Mate

Meredith Corporation

Chairman and Chief Executive Officer: William T. Kerr
President and Chief Operating Officer: Stephen M. Lacy

In Memoriam: E.T. Meredith III (1933-2003)

Copyright © 2005 by Meredith Corporation, Des Moines, Iowa. First Edition.
All rights reserved. Printed in the United States of America.
Library of Congress Control Number: 2004112911
ISBN: 0-696-22409-7

Note to Readers: Due to differing conditions, tools, and individual skills, Meredith Corporation and McGraw Media assume no responsibility for any damages, injuries suffered, or losses inclurred as a result of following the information in this book. Always read and observe all of the safety precautions provided by manufactureres of any tools, equipment, or supplies, and follow all accepted safety procedures.

Contents

Why I Wrote This Book

Did you know that shaving cream is a wonderful carpet stain remover? Or that mayonnaise is a good wood cleaner and conditioner? How about clearing a slow drain with baking soda and vinegar? Sometimes you need to fix things with what you have available to you at the time. I've written this book to help you find ways to reuse, repurpose, and recycle things around the house and give them a second, third or even fourth life! As you'll learn in this book, you'll save yourself time and money—and get a great feeling of accomplishment—when you cleverly put products you already have in your cupboards to practical new uses.

I am very excited about sharing this book with you. It is a wonderful resource designed to help you use everyday items to fix things around your home. For instance, let's say you tried a new shampoo and didn't like it for your hair; check out p. 96 to find some easy ways to put that shampoo to work! Sick of that slimy mess left behind by your steel-wool soap pads? See p. 19 to find out how aluminum foil can help. (Hint: You also can use foil to wrap up your paintbrush. If you have to stop in the middle of a project, it eliminates multiple cleanups!) I've also created
> a quick-read chart so you can easily solve common household problems
> a handy tool section to get you familiar and comfortable working with tools.

I love sharing my tips and helping solve problems! And I've gained my knowledge through years of practice. I don't write "honey-do" lists because, well, my honey is my Mr. Break-It! He is successful in his own right but not very handy when it comes to home repairs. That's how I became Mrs. Fixit! It took so much time and energy, not to mention money, to hire someone to come in and make those small repairs that I started fixin' it myself! And lovin' it! Once I started fixing things and sharing my experiences, I found out many of my friends were in the same situation. We are all so busy these days, juggling work, family, and friends and trying to keep everything running smoothly at home. Sometimes it's just easier to do it yourself. And it's certainly cheaper.

Yes, you can do it! I'm here to empower you—and help you save time and money at the same time. My first book *Mrs. Fixit Easy Home Repair* encompassed home repairs and household hints, touching on all aspects of fixing and cleaning. As I traveled around the country, everyone I spoke to wanted more information about alternative uses and repurposing for items around the home. That's how this book was born. If you're already handy—or even if not—and are looking for some new ways to do things, I'm here for you. If you have a household problem to solve—from carpet stains to paint spills and everything in between—this book will help you solve it with an easy-to-reach product that you already have on your shelf.

Think of me, Mrs. Fixit, as the next-door neighbor you wish you had—a friend who's always there with a little know-how, tips on the right tools, and an infectious can-do attitude. As you'll see in this book, I'll give you the knowledge that you need to tackle and fix those everyday problems that crop up in your home. (And if you can't find what you're looking for in this book, see my website at www.mrsfixit.com and you can ask me directly! I'll always be just a click away.)

No longer do you have to wait for someone to come to your rescue for home repairs and household problems. Let me help save you time and money with quick and easy-to-follow household hints and tool tips.

Remember, I'm here to help you realize it really is "just that simple!"

Mrs. Fixit

ALTERNATIVE USES

✳ ✳ ✳ ✳ ✳ ✳ ✳ ✳

Have you ever been stuck

with a stain, dealt a dilemma,

posed with a problem?

Products in your home have

alternative uses that will perform

in a pinch! "It's just that simple!"

✳ ✳ ✳ ✳ ✳ ✳ ✳ ✳

Alternative Uses Reference Chart

CHALLENGES	PRODUCT, PAGE	CHALLENGES	PRODUCT, PAGE
Clean & Shine		Concrete	Kitty Litter, 69
Aluminum	Cream of Tartar, 52	Cooktop, Glass	Toothpaste, 105
Appliances	Paste Wax, 85	Copper	Lemons, 71
Bathtub	Car-Washing Mitt, 34	Countertops	Aluminum Foil, 19
	Dishwasher Detergent, 56		Baby Wipes, 22
			Borax, 28
Blender	Ice, 68	Crystal	Lemons, 71
Brick Fireplace	Dishwasher Detergent, 90	Dishes	Baking Soda, 24
	Oven Cleaner, 82		Onion Bags, 81
	Whitewall Tire Cleaner, 116		Shampoo, 96
		Dishwasher	Lemonade Mix, 70
Cabinets	Dishwasher Detergent, 56		Vinegar, 112
	Tea, 102	Electronic Equipment	
			Baby Wipes, 22
Can Opener	Waxed Paper, 115	Faucets and Fixtures	
Carpet	Baby Wipes, 22		Baby Wipes, 22
	Club Soda, 40		Dryer Sheets, 57
	Cornstarch, 48		Toothpaste, 105
	Hair Spray, 66	Floors	Car-Washing Mitt, 34
	Shaving Cream, 97		Liquid Fabric Softener, 73
	Waterless Hand Cleaner, 90		Nail Polish Remover, 78
	Window Cleaner, 90		Penetrating Oil, 87
Cast Iron	Club Soda, 40	Furniture	Cotton Balls, 49
	Olive Oil, 80	Garbage Disposal	Ice, 68
	Sand, 95	Garlic Press	Toothpicks, 106
China	Baking Soda, 24	Glass Tabletops	Liquid Fabric Softener, 73
Chrome	Baby Wipes, 22	Glassware	Denture Tablets, 53
	Dryer Sheets, 57		Oven Cleaner, 82
	Toothpaste, 105		Rice, 91
	Vodka, 113		Salt, 94
Coffee Grinder	Rice, 91		Toothpaste, 90

Alternative Uses Reference Chart

CHALLENGES	PRODUCT, PAGE	CHALLENGES	PRODUCT, PAGE
Grater	Toothpicks, 106		Toothpaste, 90
Grout	Baking Soda, 24	Silverware	Onion bags, 81
	Borax, 28	Stainless Steel	Club Soda, 40
	Dishwasher Detergent, 56		Paper Towels, 84
			Paste Wax, 85
	Whitewall Tire Cleaner, 116	Stovetop	Whitewall Tire Cleaner, 116
Leather	Cornstarch, 48	Switchplates	Lemons, 71
Marble	Cream of Tartar, 52	Teapot	Aluminum Foil, 19
	Hydrogen Peroxide, 67		Cola, 44
Microwave	Dish Soap, 55	Toilets	Borax, 28
	Vinegar, 112		Cola, 44
Mirrors	Cheesecloth, 37		Denture Tablets, 53
	Coffee Filters, 43		Dishwasher Detergent, 56
	Dryer Sheets, 57		
	Rubbing Alcohol, 93		Lemonade Mix, 70
	Tea, 102	Toothbrushes	Denture Tablets, 53
	Vodka, 113	Upholstered Furniture	
Paintbrushes	Aluminum Foil, 19		Baby Wipes, 22
Pans, Bakeware	Cola, 44		Club Soda, 40
	Dryer Sheets, 57		Shaving Cream, 97
	Oven Cleaner, 82	Vases	Denture Tablets, 53
Piano Keys (Ivory)	Yogurt, 117		Rice and vinegar, 91
Porcelain	Cream of Tartar, 52	Wallpaper	Baby Powder, 114
	Hydrogen Peroxide, 67		Bread, 29
Refrigerator	Nylons, 79	Walls	Baby Wipes, 22
	Vinegar, 109		Baking Soda, 24
Salt Shaker	Cream of Tartar, 52		Bread, 29
Shower	Car-Washing Mitt, 34		Dishwasher Detergent, 56
	Dishwasher Detergent, 56		
			Hair Dryer, 65
Silver	Aluminum Foil, 19		Rubbing Alcohol, 93
	Socks, 99		Toothpaste, 105

Alternative Uses Reference Chart

CHALLENGES	PRODUCT, PAGE	CHALLENGES	PRODUCT, PAGE
Windows	Dish Soap, 55	Food Covers	Shower Caps, 96
	Oven Cleaner, 82	Food Scraps	Bags, 23
Window Screens	Nylons, 79	Fried Food	Bags, 23
Wood Furniture	Baby Oil, 20	Fruits and Vegetables	
	Baking Soda, 24		Baking Soda, 24
	Cornstarch, 48		Gum, 64
	Mayonnaise, 75		Vegetable Peeler, 110
	Toothpaste, 105	Herbs	Cheesecloth, 37
Woodwork	Baby Wipes, 22		Coffee Filter, 43
	Baking Soda, 24	Lemon Juice	Lemons, 71
	Borax, 28	Meat	Beer, 26
	Dishwasher Detergent, 56	Pancakes	Turkey Baster, 107
	Penetrating Oil, 87	Popcorn	Bags, 23
			Cooking Oil Spray, 45
Cook		Salad Bowls	Olive Oil, 80
Baking	Cinnamon, 38	**Decorate**	
Basting	Paintbrush, 83	Artwork	Wallpaper Books, 114
Bread	Tiles, 104	Bookends	Money Matters, 77
	Twist Ties, 108	Bulletin Board	Cork Rolls, 46
Brown Sugar, Fresh			Corks, 47
	Bread, 29	Candles	Candle Wax, 30
Butter	Vegetable Peeler, 110		Crayons, 51
Buttermilk, Substitute			Vegetable Peeler, 110
	Cream of Tartar, 52	Chalk/Pencil Drawing	
Cheese	Vegetable Peeler, 110		Hair Spray, 66
Chocolate	Vegetable Peeler, 110	Doorstop	Money Matters, 77
Coffee	Paper Towels, 84	Drawers	Wallpaper Book, 114
	Salt, 94	Fabric Dye	Coffee, 41
	Vanilla, 109	Flower Arrangements	
Cookies, Fresh	Bread, 29		Food Coloring, 60
Cookware, Season	Olive Oil, 80		Hair Spray, 66
Cutting Boards	Olive Oil, 80		Salt, 94
Eggs	Turkey Baster, 107		

Alternative Uses Reference Chart

CHALLENGES	PRODUCT, PAGE
Hang Artwork	Corks, 47
	Tape, 101
Paint	Car-Washing Mitt, 34
	Nylons, 79
	Socks, 99
Place Mats	Wallpaper Books, 114
Window Treatment	Clothespins, 39

Defog

CHALLENGES	PRODUCT, PAGE
Mirrors	Dish Soap, 55
	Hair Dryer, 65

Deodorize

CHALLENGES	PRODUCT, PAGE
Air Freshener	Bar Soap, 25
Antiques	Cotton Balls, 49
Basement	Kitty Litter, 69
Bedding	Baking Soda, 24
Books	Baby Powder, 21
	Dryer Sheets, 57
Carpets	Baking Soda, 24
Car Seats	Dryer Sheets, 57
Diaper Pails	Dryer Sheets, 57
Fireplace	Baking Soda, 24
Furniture	Baking Soda, 24
Garbage Cans	Kitty Litter, 69
Gym Bags	Dryer Sheets, 57
Hampers	Baking Soda, 24
Paint Fumes	Vanilla, 109
Planters and Vases	Charcoal, 36
Refrigerator	Baking Soda, 24
	Charcoal, 36
	Coffee Grounds, 41
	Cotton Balls, 49
	Vanilla, 109
	Yogurt Container, 117

CHALLENGES	PRODUCT, PAGE
Shoes, Sneakers	Cornstarch, 48
	Dryer Sheets, 57
Undersink Cabinet	Charcoal, 36
Vacuum Bag	Cinnamon, 38
	Dryer Sheets, 57
	Vanilla, 109
Workshop	Kitty Litter, 69

Dispose

CHALLENGES	PRODUCT, PAGE
Latex Paint	Kitty Litter, 69

Dust

CHALLENGES	PRODUCT, PAGE
Candles	Rubbing Alcohol, 93
Control	Tea Bags, 102
Dust Cloth Substitute	
	Cheesecloth, 37
	Coffee Filters, 43
	Nylons, 79
Dustcover	Pillowcase, 89
Furnishings	Dryer Sheets, 57
	Socks, 99
Glass-Front Cabinet	
	Cotton Swabs, 50
Tight Spaces	Paintbrush, 83

Fireplace

CHALLENGES	PRODUCT, PAGE
Fire Starters	Bags, 23
	Candle Stubs, 30
	Cardboard Tubes, 32

Garage Chores

CHALLENGES	PRODUCT, PAGE
Vehicle Cleaning	Aluminum Foil, 19
	Mayonnaise, 75
	Rubbing Alcohol, 93
	Vinegar, 112
	Whitewall Tire Cleaner, 116

Alternative Uses Reference Chart

CHALLENGES	PRODUCT, PAGE	CHALLENGES	PRODUCT, PAGE
Vehicle Protection	Carpet Scraps, 33	Watering	Coffee Cans, 42
	Money Matters, 77		Garden Hose, 62
	Tennis Balls, 103	Weeding	Vegetable Peeler, 110
	Waxed Paper, 115	**Gift Giving**	
Garden Chores		Gift Wrap	Bags, 23
Control Fungus	Cinnamon, 38		Wallpaper Books, 114
Cut Flowers	Hydrogen Peroxide, 67	**Health**	
	Vinegar, 112	Bandage Residue	Peanut Butter, 86
	Vodka, 113	Cuts or Injury	Lip Balm, 72
Enrich Soil	Beer, 26		Rubber Gloves, 92
	Coffee, 41	Food Safety	Ice, 68
	Tea, 102	Insect Bites	Bar Soap, 25
Houseplants	Olive Oil, 80	**Holidays**	
	Shower Cap, 96	Christmas Tree	Cotton Balls, 49
	Turkey Baster, 107		Diapers, 54
Potting Plants	Bar Soap, 25		Petroleum Jelly, 88
	Diapers, 54		Turkey Baster, 107
	Sand, 95	Halloween Treats	Crayons, 51
	Tiles, 104	Luminarias	Rice, 91
	Yogurt, 117	Ornaments	Egg Cartons, 58
Seeding	Coffee Cans, 42	Wreath	Twist Ties, 108
	Milk Jugs, 76	**Housekeeping Misc.**	
Seedlings	Egg Cartons, 58	Carpet Dents	Ice, 68
	Milk Jugs, 76	Cleaning Kit	Diapers, 54
	Yogurt Containers, 117	Door Mats	Carpet Scraps, 33
Staking	Twist Ties, 108	Measuring	Corks, 47
Tools	Garbage Cans, 61		Money Matters, 77
	Penetrating Oil, 87	Pencil Substitute	Charcoal, 36
	Petroleum Jelly, 88	Rubber Band Substitute	
	Rubbing Alcohol, 93		Rubber Gloves, 92
	Sand, 95	Tape Ends	Toothpicks, 106
	Vegetable Shortening, 111	**Insulate**	
		Wall Outlets	Egg Cartons, 58

Alternative Uses Reference Chart

CHALLENGES	PRODUCT, PAGE	CHALLENGES	PRODUCT, PAGE
Jewelry Care			Hydrogen Peroxide, 67
Jewelry	Baby Powder, 21		Lemonade Mix, 70
	Club Soda, 40		Pillowcase, 89
	Denture Tablets, 53		Salt, 94
	Vodka, 113		Tennis Balls, 103
Kid Stuff			Vinegar, 112
Art Smock	Pillowcases, 89		Waterless Hand Cleaner, 90
Baby Bottles	Cardboard Carrier, 31		Window Cleaner, 90
Baby Wipes	Coffee Cans, 42	Applicators	Cotton Swabs, 50
Changing Table Pad			Paintbrush, 83
	Pillowcases, 89	**Mailing and Packaging**	
Clean Toys	Paintbrushes, 83	Packing Materials	Bags, 23
	Peanut Butter, 86		Egg Cartons, 58
Finger Paint	Food Coloring, 60	**Maintenance and Repair**	
	Yogurt, 117	Appliances	Crayons, 51
Indoor "Sandbox"	Rice, 91	Chair Seats	Hair Dryer, 65
Snacks	Yogurt, 117	Chipped Glassware	Emery Board, 59
Video Games	Address Labels, 18	Doors	Candle Stubs, 30
Label			Lip Balm, 72
Forms	Address Labels, 18		Shaving Cream, 97
Raffle Tickets	Address Labels, 18	Drains	Salt, 94
Household Objects	Address Labels, 18	Drawers	Bar Soap, 25
Packages	Candle Stubs, 30		Candle Stubs, 30
Laundry		Eyeglasses	Twist Ties, 108
Clothing	Baby Powder, 21	General	Sand, 95
and Linens	Baby Wipes, 22	Hinges	Cooking Oil Spray, 45
	Bar Soap, 25		Golf Tees, 63
	Chalk, 35	Holes	Cornstarch, 48
	Club Soda, 40		Golf Tees, 63
	Cola, 44		Steel Wool, 100
	Cream of Tartar, 52		Toothpaste, 105
	Dishwasher Detergent, 56		Toothpicks, 106

Alternative Uses Reference Chart

CHALLENGES	PRODUCT, PAGE
Inflatable Mattress	Dish Soap, 55
Floors	Baby Powder, 21
Furniture	Coffee, 41
	Crayons, 51
	Olive Oil, 80
	Shoe Polish, 98
Lightbulbs	Petroleum Jelly, 88
Locks	Cooking Oil Spray, 45
Loose Screws	Golf Tees, 63
	Lip Balm, 72
Nails	Penetrating Oil, 87
Paintbrushes	Fabric Softener, 73
Plumbing	Paste Wax, 85
Stairs	Sand, 95
Table	Money Matters, 77
Toilet Leaks	Food Coloring, 60
Windows	Bar Soap, 25
Mending & Sewing	
Beads and Pins	Coffee Filters, 43
Buttons	Money Matters, 77
Patterns	Chalk, 35
	Waxed Paper, 115
Pincushion	Steel Wool, 100
Zipper	Lip Balm, 72
	Twist Ties, 108
Moisture Control	
	Chalk, 35
	Charcoal, 36
	Cheesecloth, 37
	Coffee Filters, 43
	Onion Bags, 81
	Paper Towels, 84
	Rice, 91

CHALLENGES	PRODUCT, PAGE
Move	
Heavy Furniture	Carpet Scraps, 33
Organize	
Art Supplies	Cardboard Beverage Carrier, 31
	Egg Cartons, 58
	Yogurt Containers, 117
Cleaning Supplies	Rubber Gloves, 92
Extension Cords	Cardboard Tubes, 32
	Twist Ties, 108
Jewelry	Egg Cartons, 58
Kitchen Items	Cardboard Beverage Carrier, 31
	Cardboard Tubes, 32
	Milk Jugs, 76
Laundry Supplies	Milk Jugs, 76
Memos and Paperwork	
	Clothespins, 39
Office Supplies	Cardboard Beverage Carrier, 31
Pins	Magnets, 74
Plastic Bags	Cardboard Tubes, 32
Recipes	Clothespins, 39
Socks	Diaper Pins, 99
Sports Equipment	Garbage Cans, 61
Toiletry Items	Magnets, 74
Toys	Cardboard Beverage Carrier, 31
	Garbage Cans, 61
	Pillowcases, 89
Window Box	Tiles, 104

Alternative Uses Reference Chart

CHALLENGES	PRODUCT, PAGE
Workshop Supplies	Cardboard Beverage Carrier, 31
	Cardboard Tubes, 32
	Coffee Cans, 42
	Coffee Filters, 43
	Egg Cartons, 58
	Magnets, 74
	Milk Jugs, 76
Personal Care	
Bathing	Baby Wipes, 22
Hairbrush	Shampoo, 96
Hands and Feet	Baby Oil, 20
	Lemonade Mix, 70
	Olive Oil, 80
	Rubber Gloves, 92
	Shaving Cream, 97
Shaving Cream	Hair Conditioner, 97
Skin Care	Vegetable Shortening, 111
Pest Control	
Animals	Black Pepper, 27
	Cinnamon, 38
	Cotton Balls, 49
	Gum, 64
	Olive Oil, 80
	Petroleum Jelly, 88
	Steel Wool, 100
Insects	Baby Oil, 20
	Beer, 26
	Black Pepper, 27
	Borax, 28
	Chalk, 35
	Cheesecloth, 37

CHALLENGES	PRODUCT, PAGE
	Coffee Cans, 42
	Dish Soap, 55
	Gum, 64
	Hair Spray, 66
	Petroleum Jelly, 88
	Tape, 101
Pet Care	
Grooming	Baby Wipes, 22
	Steel Wool, 100
Preserve, Protect, Prevent	
Appliance Racks	Paste Wax, 85
China and Dishes	Cork Rolls, 46
	Paper Towels, 84
Floors	Cork Rolls, 46
	Rubber Gloves, 92
	Socks, 99
Lawn Mower Blades	
	Cooking Oil Spray, 45
Newspaper Clippings	
	Hair Spray, 66
Plastic Containers	Cooking Oil Spray, 45
Putty Knife	Cooking Oil Spray, 45
Saw Blades	Candle Stubs, 30
	Garden Hose, 62
	Penetrating Oil, 87
	Waxed Paper, 115
Saw Horse	Carpet Scraps, 33
Screws	Candle Stubs, 30
Sports Equipment	Shaving Cream, 97
Tabletops	Baby Oil, 20
	Cork Rolls, 46
	Tiles, 104

Alternative Uses Reference Chart

CHALLENGES	PRODUCT, PAGE	CHALLENGES	PRODUCT, PAGE
Tools	Carpet Scraps, 33		Mayonnaise, 75
	Cork Rolls, 46		Nail Polish Remover, 78
	Paste Wax, 85		Peanut Butter, 86
Walls	Corks, 47	Tree Sap	Baby Oil, 20
Wood Furniture	Paste Wax, 85	Wallpaper	Liquid Fabric Softener, 73
Remove		**Retrieve**	
Cloudy Residue	Vinegar, 112	Items in Grate	Gum, 64
Decals	Hair Dryer, 65	Metal Objects	Magnets, 74
Dried Glue	Emery Board, 59	**Safety**	
Dried Wood Sap	Emery Board, 59	Broken Glass	Bread, 29
Grease	Cola, 44	Broken Light Bulb	Tennis Balls, 103
Gum	Baby Oil, 20	Sharp Objects	Garden Hose, 62
	Ice, 68	Stepladder	Carpet Scraps, 33
	Peanut Butter, 86	Swing Sets	Garden Hose, 62
Lime Scale	Cola, 44	**Sanitize**	
	Lemons, 71	Mold and Mildew	Hydrogen Peroxide, 67
Rust	Cola, 44		
Melted Plastic	Nail Polish Remover, 78		
Photos	Hair Dryer, 65	**Secure Possessions**	
Rusty Bolts	Cola, 44	Small Valuables	Mayonnaise Jar, 75
Silly Putty	Penetrating Oil, 87	Suitcase	Twist Ties, 108
Soap Scum	Baby Oil, 20	**Sharpen**	
	Cooking Oil Spray, 45	Pencils	Emery Board, 59
	Vinegar, 112		Vegetable Peeler, 110
Stains	Borax, 28	**Shoe Care**	
	Cornstarch, 48	Patent Leather	Coffee Filter, 43
	Emery Board, 59		Petroleum Jelly, 88
	Hair Spray, 66	Shape	Bags, 23
	Nail Polish Remover, 78	**Sports Equipment**	
	Vegetable Shortening, 111	Fishing Bobber	Corks, 47
		Leather Mitt	Olive Oil, 80
Stickers	Hair Dryer, 65	Storage	Garbage Cans, 61
	Hydrogen Peroxide, 67		

Alternative Uses Reference Chart

CHALLENGES	PRODUCT, PAGE		CHALLENGES	PRODUCT, PAGE
Static Control			**Tools**	Rubber Gloves, 92
Carpets	Liquid Fabric Softener, 73		Woodworking	Nylons, 79
Store			**Yard Work**	
Cast Iron	Coffee Filters, 43		Gutters	Nylons, 79
	Paper Towels, 84		Lawn Mower	Turkey Baster, 107
Clothing	Garbage Cans, 61			
	Golf Tees, 63			
Dishes	Coffee Filters, 43			
Linens	Cardboard Tubes, 32			
Steel Wool	Aluminum Foil, 100			
Vacuum				
	Onion Bags, 81			
Unclog				
Drains	Cola, 44			
	Denture Tablets, 53			
Faucets	Vinegar, 112			
Spray Cans	Rubbing Alcohol, 93			
Showerheads	Lemonade Mix, 70			
Workshop Chores				
Apply Stain	Diapers, 54			
	Nylons, 79			
Glue	Cotton Swabs, 50			
Paint Can	Money Matters, 77			
	Waxed Paper, 115			
Polishing	Steel Wool, 100			
Projects	Tape, 101			
	Tennis Balls, 103			
Sanding	Emery Boards, 59			
	Tape, 101			
Strip Paint	Oven Cleaner, 82			
Tighten Screws	Money Matters, 77			
	Vegetable Peeler, 110			

Address Labels

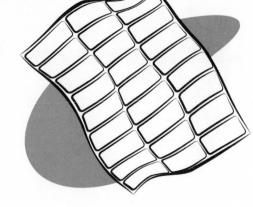

Do you find yourself with an abundance of free address labels in your mailbox from various organizations? Put them to good use.

HOUSEKEEPING

➤ Carry the labels in your handbag or car's glove compartment, and they'll be handy to give your address to a friend or to fill out a form. They are especially handy when **filling out stubs for the raffle tickets** that schoolkids sell.

➤ Stick an address label on important **items that can be misplaced easily, such as your eyeglasses case, keys, cell phone, or PDA**—these items are more likely to find their way home with your address attached.

➤ Attach an address label to the **underside of a dish before you take it to a friend's house;** this way it will be easy for the hostess to identify your dish when she is trying to return it.

KID STUFF

➤ Stick an address label on your **child's video game cartridges to make it easy for your child to identify his or her games** when playing with friends.

Aluminum Foil

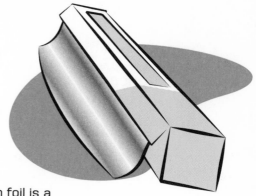

Aluminum foil is indispensable for cooking, but consider having a box handy for more than meals.

IN THE KITCHEN

➤ Take the tarnish off your teapot. Aluminum foil is a key ingredient in my favorite **silver-cleaning recipe.** Line a stainless-steel sink or large pot with aluminum foil (shiny side up), sprinkle 2 to 4 tablespoons of baking soda over the foil, and fill the sink or pot with boiling water. Put on rubber gloves, dip the silver pieces in, and watch the tarnish disappear right before your eyes!

> **TIP:** *Always be extra careful around superhot water. Protect your hands with thick rubber gloves—you'll keep a good grip on your silver pieces and keep the hot water away from your skin.*

➤ **Eliminate the mess on your counter from a steel wool soap pad.** Wrap the pad in foil and pop it in the freezer after each use—you won't have to deal with the slimy mess and the pad won't rust!

HOME CARE & REPAIR

➤ If you need to stop in the middle of a painting project, **there is no need to clean the brushes until you're finished with the job.** Wrap your paintbrush in aluminum foil and stash it in the freezer. When you're ready to continue painting, simply pull it out, let it warm to room temperature, and keep painting— only one cleanup per project.

IN THE GARAGE

➤ If the chrome hubcaps on your favorite vehicle have become downright cruddy, use a balled-up piece of aluminum foil (shiny side out) to **polish your hubcaps** to a shine!

Baby Oil

A good all-purpose oil,
baby oil really isn't just for babies!

IN THE BATH

➤ **Keep soap scum from building up on shower curtains** by coating them with a little baby oil.

➤ Baby oil can help **break through hardened soap scum on bathtubs and tile.** Just put some on a washcloth and scrub the tub area clean.

> TIP: *Be sure to thoroughly rinse away all the baby oil from the tub floor, and keep the baby oil on the shower curtain—not dripping into the tub. Baby oil is slippery! Use a little shampoo to break up the oil.*

PERSONAL CARE

➤ Use baby oil to **clean paint from your skin.** Just rub it in and the paint will slide off.

➤ Rub baby oil on your hands to **dissolve tree sap**. You can also rub it on household surfaces to remove sap.

➤ Baby oil can also be **used as a mosquito deterrent.** Just rub it on exposed skin.

HOUSEKEEPING

➤ **Use a little baby oil instead of furniture polish.** It's inexpensive and leaves a beautiful shine.

➤ Baby oil can be used to **remove a dish or glass stuck to your tabletop.** Squirt some baby oil around the base of the dish and let it sit for a few minutes; the dish should then pull off easily.

KID STUFF

If your **child has gum in his or her hair,** saturate the area with baby oil and gently comb out the gum.

Baby Powder

Beyond protecting little ones, baby powder has some surprising uses around the house, so keep a bottle nearby.

HOME CARE & REPAIR

➤ **Stop floorboard squeaks.** Sprinkle some baby powder on your wood floors and sweep it back and forth, working it into the cracks; sweep away any excess. The squeaks will be silenced!

HOUSEKEEPING

➤ **Get rid of that musty smell.** Sprinkle baby powder between the pages of musty-smelling books. Let the books sit for a few hours to a few days depending on just how musty they smell. Then simply sweep out the powder with a soft paintbrush.

STAIN REMOVAL

➤ Use baby powder to **keep a grease stain from setting into fabric.** Sprinkle the powder onto the stain, let it absorb for a few minutes, and then brush it off.

PERSONAL CARE

➤ **Release a knot in a necklace.** Put the necklace on a plate and sprinkle some baby powder over the chain. Then use two needles to work the knot apart. The powder works as a lubricant.

A B C D E F G H I J K L M N O P Q R S T U V W X Y Z

Baby Wipes

Beyond keeping the baby clean, baby wipes go a long way toward keeping the house clean.

HOUSEKEEPING

➤ **Run a wipe over your pet's coat to remove loose fur** before it ends up all over the carpets and furniture. To pick up pet fur that's already on carpet and upholstery, just run a baby wipe over it.

➤ Keep a box under the bathroom sink to use to **quickly clean counters and chrome fixtures.**

➤ Baby wipes will also **clean electronic equipment such as televisions, stereos, and computers**.

> TIP: Be sure to use baby wipes WITHOUT lanolin on your electronics and counters— lanolin can leave a sticky film.

STAIN REMOVAL

➤ **Stop a stain before it sets on your clothes.** If you spill something, grab a wipe. It will clean up the mess and help keep the stain from setting until you can wash it.

➤ **Get rid of deodorant stains on clothes.** Don't start looking for a new outfit; just wipe the stain away!

➤ **Clean crayon marks off walls and woodwork** with a wipe and a little elbow grease.

PERSONAL CARE

➤ Freshen up without a sink and water. Just grab a baby wipe; it gently cleans and removes makeup.

Bags

Grocery bags, lunch bags, shopping bags—every time you turn around there's another bag to deal with! Well, I have some great ways to repurpose those bags!

PROJECTS
➤ They make great free **packing materials when sending out packages or packing for a move.**

➤ Use your home paper shredder to cut paper bags into inexpensive **filler for gift bags and packages!**

PERSONAL CARE
➤ Plastic grocery bags can be **stuffed into boots and handbags to help them retain their shape** in storage.

IN THE KITCHEN
➤ Dump your homemade french fries or air-popped popcorn into a brown paper shopping bag, put in your salt or butter or whatever else you want, seal the top, and shake! The bag will **absorb excess oil from fried foods and popcorn, and it's large enough to coat everything easily!**

HOUSEKEEPING
➤ Use a paper bag to **collect food scraps after you eat.** Line a big bowl with a plastic grocery bag and scrape scraps directly into the bag, tie it up, and toss it out with the trash.

Mrs. Fixit's AMAZING!

Stuff a brown paper bag with crumpled newspaper, seal it up at the end and use it as kindling in your fireplace. Your bag log will burn longer than plain paper to catch the logs on fire, ensuring a good, strong fire!

Home Care Tip

Baking Soda

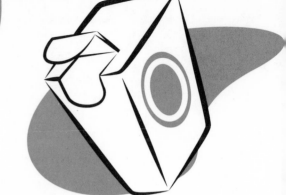

Baking soda is a must-have in any household. It can be used in every room in the house—really!

IN THE KITCHEN

➤ **Keep the fridge smelling fresh** with an open box on a shelf. When you change the box every three to six months, dump the old soda down your kitchen sink or disposal to deodorize your drain.

➤ **Clean dirt and residue off fresh fruits and vegetables;** just sprinkle some baking soda on a damp cloth and rub away.

➤ Give your dish soap a kick. Add a couple of tablespoons to help **cut through grease and grime in your dishwater.**

HOUSEKEEPING

➤ Baking soda can **absorb odors on upholstered furniture.** You can also **sprinkle it in the fireplace, on carpets, in laundry hampers, and on bedding for the same refreshing effect.**

STAIN REMOVAL

➤ **Clean the grout in the bathroom**—and bring it back to its original white—with a mix of baking soda and hydrogen peroxide.

➤ If your little Picasso used an indelible marker on wood furniture, **remove the marker stains** by dipping a damp cloth in baking soda and wiping them away!

➤ Mix baking soda with a little water to **remove coffee and tea stains from your good china.**

Bar Soap

You might never have thought that a plain bar of soap could be used everywhere from the laundry room to the workshop. Well, it can—here's how!

STAIN REMOVAL
➤ Keep a bar of white soap by your washing machine. It is a great **pretreater for clothing stains,** especially for removing makeup. Dampen the bar, rub it into the stain, and then wash according to directions.

➤ It will also **remove fabric softener stains**—those greasy stains on your clean laundry. Just rub some soap into the stains and launder again.

HOME CARE & REPAIR
➤ Use a bar of soap to **take the stick out of sticking drawers or windows**. Rub a bar of soap along the sliding parts to get them moving smoothly again.

➤ Soap can be **used as both an insect repellent and an air freshener.** Store bars of opened soap in drawers, closets, and suitcases.

PERSONAL CARE
➤ Soap is also indispensable in the summer to **help relieve the pain from nasty insect bites.** Dampen the soap and rub it over your bites for an instant anesthetic effect.

➤ If you're potting houseplants or working in the garden, gently scrape your fingernails over a bar of soap to **prevent dirt and debris from getting under your nails.** It washes away easily when you're done.

Mrs. Fixit's **AMAZING!**

The best soap for cleaning is unscented white bar soap. Fancier soaps have other ingredients you don't need for household chores.

Home Care Tip

Beer

The ingredients in beer make it especially useful in the garden, but it has some practical indoor uses too.

IN THE GARDEN

➤ Yeast is beneficial to plants, so pour a few tablespoons of flat beer into your garden to **enrich the soil.**

➤ If bees are a problem in your yard, **create a bee trap** by punching a series of $3/8$-inch holes in the lid of an old glass or plastic jar. Fill the jar about half full with beer, screw the lid on, and place the jar in the yard where you've seen bees. Bees are attracted to the beer and will crawl through the holes in the lid to get to it—but they can't get out!

➤ **Eliminate slugs** that are sliming up your garden. Bury an empty tuna can next to your plants so just the lip is sticking out. Fill the can with beer and check it in the morning—you should have caught some of those party animals! All you have to do is empty the can each day. This trick also works with earwigs.

➤ **Keep your garden party insect-free** by placing a few open cans of beer around the perimeter of the yard. Insects are attracted to your first-line-of-defense beer border, stopping many of them before they get to your guests.

IN THE KITCHEN

➤ Speaking of a garden party, you can **tenderize a tough cut of meat** for a barbecue by marinating it for an hour or so in some beer.

Black Pepper

Wondering how an everyday staple like black pepper might help around the house? I have some ideas!

IN THE YARD

➤ Sprinkle black pepper around your yard to **keep dogs, cats, rabbits, squirrels, and raccoons away from your plants.** This also works to **keep cats out of your houseplants.**

➤ Sprinkle some pepper around your garbage can to **keep animals out of the garbage.**

HOUSEKEEPING

➤ Wrap black peppercorns, cinnamon sticks, and cloves in a piece of cheesecloth or breathable fabric and hang it in closets for an **inexpensive moth repellent.**

➤ Use pepper as an **ant deterrent**. Sprinkle pepper anywhere you've seen ants—they hate it and will stay far away.

Borax

Some of the best solutions
for pest problems, toilet troubles,
and cleaning concerns are in an
unassuming box in your laundry room.

HOUSEKEEPING

➤ **Get rid of ants and roaches** that are invading your
home. Mix together 1/2 cup borax, 1/3 cup sugar, and
1/2 cup water. Then soak up the mixture with several
cotton balls. Stash the balls in cracks and crevices or
anywhere you've seen pests. They eat it up, and that's
the end of them!

➤ **Make an all-purpose cleaner** to use on everything
from countertops to painted woodwork. Mix together
2 teaspoons borax, 2 teaspoons baking soda,
4 teaspoons lemon juice, 1/2 teaspoon dish soap, and
4 cups hot water. Put the mixture in a squirt bottle and
use it as a **stain remover in the laundry room.** You
can fight tough stains such as fruit juice, red wine,
colored alcohol, and chocolate. Simply squirt, rub in, let
sit an hour or so, and then wash.

➤ Need a little scrubbing power? All you have to do is
combine 2 cups baking soda, 2 cups borax, and 2 cups
salt. Use the concoction to **scour away stains
without scratching surfaces.** Plus, you can store it in
an airtight container so it is ready to go when you are.

STAIN REMOVAL

➤ Mix a paste of borax and lemon juice to **remove
toilet or grout stains.** Spread it over the stains, let
it sit for about 15 minutes, and then scrub those
stains away.

Bread

White bread, that lunch box staple, can help you in other ways around the house.

STAIN REMOVAL

➤ Pull off the crusts and mold a slice of bread into a little ball; then use the ball to **rub scuffs and stains off of wallpaper and paint.**

HOME CARE & REPAIR

➤ If you've ever broken a glass you know it takes forever to get those little shards off the floor. Carefully pick up all of the big pieces and put them in a paper bag. Then use a slice of bread to **pick up the small shards of glass.** They'll get caught in the bread for safe and easy cleanup.

IN THE KITCHEN

➤ If your brown sugar has turned as hard as a rock, stick a piece of fresh bread into the same airtight container and close it for a couple of days. The bread will **soften the brown sugar.**

➤ **Keep cookies fresher longer** by placing a piece of white bread in the bottom of the cookie jar.

Mrs. Fixit's **AMAZING!**

White bread works best! Whole-grain breads won't work the same way for most uses.

Home Care Tip

Candle Stubs

Save those candle stubs; you'll be able to put them to good use around the house with these easy "stub-stitutions!"

HOUSEKEEPING

➤ The stub of an old candle is the perfect tool for **freeing up sticking drawers.** Just rub the wax along the moving parts of the drawer and watch the drawer slide easily into place. This same treatment also works on stubborn windows!

➤ Candle stubs are perfect **fire starters in the fireplace or at the campsite.** Light the candle and hold it in place long enough to light your kindling without burning your fingers!

➤ Rub a white candle stub over the label on a package before you ship. The candle will **seal in the ink and protect the address on the package.**

➤ Use candle wax to **help a candle stand up in a candleholder.** Drip some wax into the bottom of the holder and press the new candle into place. As the wax cools, it will hold the candle in place.

HOME CARE & REPAIR

➤ Use a candle to **silence the squeak from a door.** Carefully remove the hinge pin, rub the stub of a candle all over it, and slip it back in place. The squeak will be gone.

IN THE WORKSHOP

➤ You can use the stubs to **coat screws and saw blades so they will easily move through wood.**

Cardboard Beverage Carrier

These clever little carriers do more than get drink bottles home from the store—they're the perfect "extra set of hands" to carry lots of small items.

IN THE KITCHEN
➤ To **set the table**, load up the compartments with silverware, napkins, and salt and pepper shakers. This way you won't have to make 10 trips to the kitchen. Come back and reload with glasses or condiments. This trick also works great for summertime barbecues.

KID CARE
➤ If you have an infant in the house, these carriers are perfect for **organizing baby bottles** in the refrigerator. It will keep them all together so you don't have to dig around when you need one.

HOUSEKEEPING
➤ **Organize arts and crafts supplies**—paintbrushes, ribbons, glue sticks, and wire cutters—whatever you need will be right where you need it. This also works for pens, pencils, scissors, and staplers on a desktop, and in a child's room to **coordinate all those little stuffed beanbag toys** in one place.

Mrs. Fixit's AMAZING!

If you don't like the look of the cardboard, you can always spray-paint or cover it with contact paper, but because it's serving as an extra hand, there's really no need.

Design Tip

A B C D E F G H I J K L M N O P Q R S T U V W X Y Z

Cardboard Tubes
(Paper Towel, Toilet Paper, Wrapping Paper)

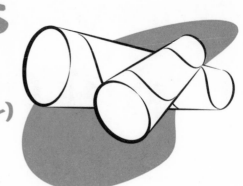

Don't toss those tubes! Cardboard tubes can help organize all sorts of things around the house.

IN THE WORKSHOP
➤ Use toilet paper tubes to **protect the blades of your chisels and keep them sharp.**

IN THE KITCHEN
➤ **Keep your knives nice and sharp** by flattening some paper towel tubes and slipping your knives into them.

HOME CARE & REPAIR
➤ **Prevent your extension cords from getting tangled.** Coil them and slip them through a paper towel tube to keep them corralled and neat.

➤ Roll up newspaper and slip inside a paper towel tube to **use as kindling "logs" for your fireplace.**

HOUSEKEEPING
➤ **Make a sturdy base to hang your linens** so you don't get a hanger crease and end up ironing again. Make sure that your table linens are pressed. Then, cut a slit down the length of two paper towel tubes, slip them inside of each other, and put them on the long part of a hanger.

➤ **Keep plastic grocery bags from piling up** all over the place. Stuff them inside a cardboard tube to keep them neat and organized.

Carpet Scraps

There are always scraps left after carpet is installed. Keep a few pieces in storage in case you ever need a patch—but the rest can go to good use around the house.

IN THE GARAGE

➤ Hang a patch of carpet on the wall in your garage where your car door opens. The carpet will **protect your car door from dings and scratches** when you open the door too fast and hit the wall.

HOME CARE & REPAIR

➤ Put some carpet (pile side down) on a hardwood floor when you **move heavy furniture.** Place the furniture on top of the carpet and slide it easily without scratching wood, tile, or vinyl flooring.

➤ Larger scraps make perfect **throw rugs by the back door to wipe your feet.**

IN THE WORKSHOP

➤ Put some carpet across the top of your sawhorse to **protect projects from scuffs and scratches.**

➤ **Line the inside of a tool drawer** with carpet scraps. Tools will stay in place when the drawer is opened, instead of sliding around and getting damaged.

Mrs. Fixit's

AMAZING!

Cut a piece of carpet to size and staple it on the bottom rung of your ladder. You can wipe your feet before you climb up so you'll be less likely to slip.

Home Care & Repair Tip

Car-Washing Mitts

Those big fuzzy cotton car-washing mitts at your local home center are great for all kinds of cleaning jobs. Grab a bunch; they are great to have around the house.

HOUSEKEEPING

➤ Spray your mitt with furniture dusting polish for a **quick cleanup job on furniture and woodwork.** Better yet, put one on each hand and get the job done twice as fast!

> **TIP:** *Get your kids to help with the housework by giving them a pair of mitts and putting them to work.*

➤ They are great for **cleaning large surfaces, such as showers, tubs and floors.** Pull on a rubber glove, then the mitt, and go to work!

HOME CARE & REPAIR

➤ You can also use these mitts to **apply a decorative paint technique** called "ragging," which will add character to your walls. These mitts cost a fraction of the price of "specialty" painting gloves.

Chalk

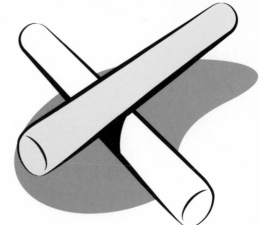

Chalk has so many great uses, and it's as easy as 1-2-3 to use.

STAIN REMOVAL

➤ To **remove a grease stain or a little ring around the collar,** grab some chalk. Rub it into the stain, let it sit for a few minutes, dust it off, and launder as usual. The chalk dust will get into the fibers and absorb the oils that are causing the stain.

HOME CARE & REPAIR

➤ Put a bundle of chalk sticks in your closets and cabinets to **absorb moisture and keep items from getting damp and musty.**

➤ Wrap a small bundle of chalk in cheesecloth, tie it off, and **store it with your silver to keep the pieces from tarnishing.** The chalk absorbs excess moisture, which can speed up the tarnishing process.

IN THE WORKSHOP

➤ A bundle of chalk in your toolbox will help **keep your tools from rusting.**

HOUSEKEEPING

➤ To **keep ants out of your house,** draw chalk lines around your doorways and windowsills. The ants won't cross the chalk line.

IN THE GARDEN

➤ Powdered chalk scattered around garden plants is a good **repellent for ants and slugs.**

Mrs. Fixit's
AMAZING!

Next time you need to trace a pattern, use chalk. It will be easy to see and you can simply dust away the lines when you're finished.

Project Tip

Charcoal

If you have a bag of charcoal for the grill in your garage, you can put it to use for more than just barbecuing!

IN THE KITCHEN

➤ To **keep undersink cabinets from smelling musty,** fill an onion bag with charcoal and hang it from a cup hook on the "roof" of the cabinet. Your little sachet will absorb odors and control moisture.

➤ A dish of charcoal will **keep the fridge smelling good** too.

IN THE WORKSHOP

➤ Keep a charcoal briquette in your toolbox to **keep tools from rusting.**

HOUSEKEEPING

➤ Crush a few briquettes and sprinkle in the bottom of planters, terrariums, and vases before adding plants and flowers. The charcoal will **kill germs and neutralize odors.**

➤ In a pinch you can use a piece of charcoal **in place of a pencil** if you can't find one.

Cheesecloth

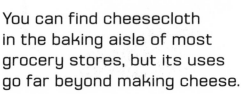
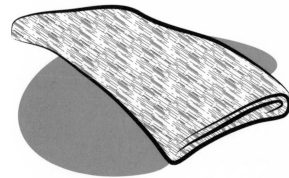

You can find cheesecloth in the baking aisle of most grocery stores, but its uses go far beyond making cheese.

HOUSEKEEPING

➤ **Use cheesecloth anytime you need a lint-free cloth**—from washing windows and mirrors to dusting to sanding and staining in the workshop. These cloths will get the job done quickly and inexpensively.

➤ **Repel moths that can wreak havoc on clothes and linens.** Mix together ¼ cup whole cloves and ¼ cup black peppercorns. Add several cinnamon sticks broken into small pieces. Wrap the mixture in cheesecloth and hang in closets or stash in drawers to keep moths at bay.

> TIP: *Look for a cheesecloth with a tightly woven fabric to hold things in.*

IN THE KITCHEN
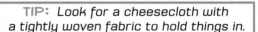

➤ **Add great flavor to your favorite recipes.** Wrap fresh herbs in cheesecloth, tie it off with a piece of string, and dunk it into your recipes. When the dish is done, simply remove the entire bundle. You get all of the flavor and none of those woody stalks and stems!

Cinnamon

Sweet-smelling cinnamon is useful
for more than baking.

IN THE YARD

➤ Cinnamon sticks can **prevent cats and dogs from
chewing leaves and digging up soil.** Bury some
sticks just under the soil to keep the critters at bay.

➤ Sprinkle some cinnamon around the base of your
peony plants to help **prevent fungus growth.**

➤ Sprinkle some around the perimeter of your yard
each week to **keep neighborhood cats and
dogs away.**

IN THE KITCHEN

➤ **Cinnamon can help when you run out of allspice
while baking.** Mix 1½ teaspoons each ground cloves
and ground cinnamon to equal 1 tablespoon of allspice.

HOUSEKEEPING

➤ Pop a few cinnamon sticks into your vacuum bag
to **spread their spicy, fresh scent throughout the
house** when you're cleaning!

Clothespins

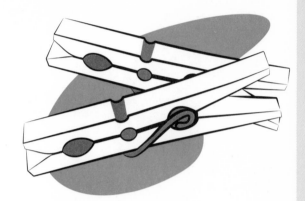

Clip-on clothespins are great
to have on hand.

HOUSEKEEPING/ORGANIZATION
➤ Use a clothespin to **clip together paperwork**
when you can't find a paper clip.

➤ Glue a magnet to the back and use it
to **clip pictures and memos on the fridge!**

➤ Use some clothespins to **hang a series
of vintage dish towels across your window**
for a whimsical window treatment.

IN THE KITCHEN
➤ Use a clothespin to **clip a recipe to the
handle on your kitchen cabinets.** The recipe
will be right at eye level and won't get messy
while you're cooking.

IN THE WORKSHOP
➤ **Use clothespins as a clamp** for small projects.

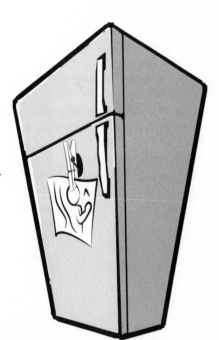

Club Soda

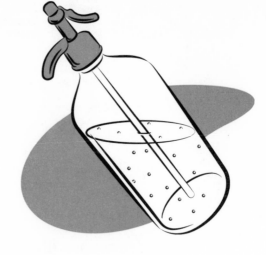

This inexpensive little gem of a product can remove stains, shine surfaces, and clean cookware—among other things!

PERSONAL CARE

➤ **Clean your gemstone jewelry** with club soda—it does a beautiful job. Just put some club soda in a glass with your jewelry and let it soak overnight. Wipe with a clean, dry cloth in the morning.

IN THE KITCHEN

➤ **Keep food from sticking to cast-iron cookware.** To avoid a big mess in your pan, pour in some club soda while the pan is still warm. It will prevent food from sticking and make cleanup a lot easier.

➤ Use club soda to **shine stainless-steel surfaces** such as pots and pans, sinks, and faucets.

STAIN REMOVAL

➤ Club soda is an **amazing stain remover on clothes, carpets, and upholstery.** Simply take a white cloth and pour a little club soda on the cloth. Dab the cloth directly on stains such as wine, grease, fruit, and chocolate. When you see that the stain is lifting, dab with a clean cloth and cool water.

Coffee

Coffee is a morning, noon, and night staple at my house because it has so many great alternative uses.

HOME CARE & REPAIR

➤ To **eliminate scratches on dark wood furniture,** make a paste of instant coffee and water. Rub the paste into the scratch with a soft cloth, then let it sit for a minute. Buff away any excess.

PLANT CARE

➤ For acid-loving plants such as gardenias, hibiscus, and azaleas, sprinkle some coffee grounds on the soil around the plant. The grounds **add acidity to the soil.**

HOUSEKEEPING

➤ Coffee grounds can come in handy in the fridge. Poke some holes in a plastic container, fill it with used coffee grounds, then stick it in the fridge. The grounds will help **eliminate odors.**

➤ Strong black coffee can be used to **dye fabric.** Soak fabric in a bucket of coffee overnight. In the morning, launder on the delicate cycle without detergent, but do add 1 cup of white vinegar to set the color.

Mrs. Fixit's AMAZING!

Flavored coffee? Put a few drops of your favorite flavored extract (vanilla, peppermint, hazelnut) into the coffee grounds before you brew. You'll get a great gourmet flavor!

Taste Tip

Coffee Cans

Empty coffee cans are just the right size and shape for lots of jobs around the house.

IN THE WORKSHOP
➤ **Use coffee cans in the workshop** for everything from soaking paintbrushes to organizing nails and screws.

IN THE YARD
➤ For an easy way to **spread grass seed,** just grab a large coffee can. Use a nail to punch several holes in the bottom, as well as two holes across from each other near the top. Put a string through the holes near the top to make yourself an easy handle, and put the plastic cover over the holes on the bottom of the can. Fill the can with grass seed, remove the cover, and shake the can around the yard.

➤ Put a coffee can on your lawn to use as an easy **gauge to make sure you've watered the lawn enough.** Put a coffee can or plastic dish in the path of your sprinkler. You'll want about an inch of water on your lawn.

HOME CARE & REPAIR
➤ Bugs are attracted to moisture; fill old coffee cans with salt, kitty litter, or charcoal, and put them around the basement. This will soak up excess moisture and help **prevent the bugs from breeding.**

KID CARE
➤ To **make homemade baby wipes,** cut a roll of paper towels in half so you end up with two halves that look like toilet paper rolls. Put them in a large, clean coffee can. Mix 1½ cups water and 1 tablespoon each of baby shampoo and baby oil. Pour it over the towels and let them soak. When they're good and wet, extract the center cardboard core and pull your homemade wipes easily one by one.

Coffee Filters

Those inexpensive little filters can do so much more than keep coffee grounds in place.

HOUSEKEEPING

➤ When **stacking your good china for storage** put a flattened flat-bottom coffee filter between each plate; it absorbs any moisture left on the plates and prevents the plates from chipping.

➤ **Use filters between freshly cleaned cast-iron skillets** to absorb excess moisture.

➤ Coffee filters are good **lint-free cleaning cloths;** use them for dusting or cleaning windows and mirrors.

➤ Another no-lint cleanup idea: Use a coffee filter to **apply shoe polish!**

IN THE KITCHEN

➤ A coffee filter makes the **perfect container for a bouquet garni**—a bundle of fresh herbs that you use like a tea bag when cooking soups and stews. Simply put the herbs inside the filter, tie it closed with some kitchen string, and tie the little bag to the pot handle for easy retrieval. Just be sure the tail of the string isn't so long that it reaches the burner.

HOME CARE & REPAIR

➤ Use a series of coffee filters to **keep track of materials while working on a project,** such as nails and screws, beads, or pins.

Cola

Keep a few cans of cola in your refrigerator because it can help with all sorts of household tasks.

IN THE WORKSHOP

➤ If you need to **remove a rusty bolt or clean rust off of other metal surfaces,** it's cola to the rescue. Pour a little on a scrubbing pad and go to work. The rust will disappear in no time!

HOME CARE & REPAIR

➤ Sluggish drain? Pour some cola down there. It will bubble and fizz away greasy buildup and **keep your drains flowing smoothly.**

➤ Pour a can of cola down your toilet, wait an hour, and then **scrub away those stubborn toilet stains.**

IN THE KITCHEN

➤ **Remove cooked-on crud** by pouring some cola into your pan and bringing it to a boil. The carbonation and heat will work together to loosen the mess. This same procedure will **remove lime scale from the inside of your teapot.** Just pour it in and bring to a boil.

STAIN REMOVAL

➤ Cola is also a great degreaser. Pour it over a load of greasy work clothes, on a greasy stain in your garage, or even a nasty spill in the kitchen. It will **break up grease** so that it is easy to clean away.

Cooking Oil Spray

Cooking oil spray has made working in the kitchen a little easier, but did you know that it can help around your house?

IN THE YARD

➤ Spray the blades of your lawn mower with cooking oil spray. It will help **prevent grass from sticking to the lawn mower blades** and making a big mess.

HOME CARE & REPAIR

➤ Take care of a squeaky hinge by pulling out the pin and spraying a little cooking oil spray on it. Put the pin back in place, and the **squeaks will be eliminated.**

➤ Spritz your key with a little oil to **unstick locks.** Turn the key back and forth in the lock to lubricate the parts.

HOUSEKEEPING

➤ Keep some cooking oil spray in the bathroom to help **loosen soap scum in the shower.** Then, easily wipe it away with soap and water. Just be sure you don't get it on the floor of the shower or bathtub because it is very slippery.

IN THE KITCHEN

➤ Spritz the inside of plastic containers before storing tomato sauce. The cooking oil spray will **eliminate stains usually left behind** after you clean the containers.

➤ **Spritz butter-flavored cooking spray** on air-popped popcorn; it's less fattening than butter and tastes great too!

Mrs. Fixit's
AMAZING!

Spray your putty knife with cooking oil spray before you strip paint off of something, and it will be much easier to clean off as you work.

Shop Tip

Cork Rolls

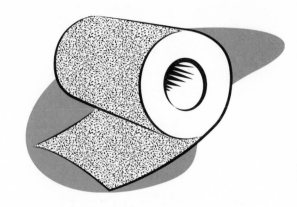

Keep a roll or two of cork at your house: It's easy to work with for several household projects.

IN THE KITCHEN

➤ High-end cabinetry often comes lined with cork to **protect the inside of your cabinets as well as your dishes.** Do it yourself. Measure the inside of a cabinet drawer, and use a straightedge and a utility knife to cut through the cork. Adhere the cork to the cabinet with double-sided carpet tape or spray adhesive.

HOUSEKEEPING

➤ Another great use for cork is to **line the bottom of lamps and vases so they don't scratch your wood furniture**. Just trace the shape of the piece onto the cork and cut it out. Then adhere it with spray adhesive.

➤ Put it on the feet of your furniture to **protect your floors,** or under a throw rug to **make a nonslip surface.**

➤ **Make a decorative bulletin board for the kitchen.** Cut the cork to fit into a standard picture frame. Insert as you would a picture and hang it near the phone to collect grocery lists, calendars, and messages.

IN THE WORKSHOP

➤ Cork also **makes a great inexpensive liner for your toolbox or workbench.**

Corks
(Wine Corks)

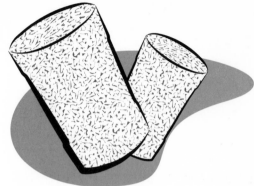

Save the corks you pop out
of those wine bottles—they're
great to have on hand.

HOUSEKEEPING

➤ Cut a cork into ⅛-inch sections. Glue the slices to the
back corners of wall-hung picture frames. The cork
**holds the picture in place and protects the wall
from damage.**

➤ Screw a cork into the back of a door to **act as a
doorstop.**

➤ Glue a bunch of corks to a piece of plywood to **make
a homemade "cork" board.**

VACATION

➤ If you have a fishing trip planned and you've run out
of bobbers, try attaching a cork from a wine bottle to
the line. The cork will make a great **substitute bobber.**

IN THE WORKSHOP

➤ If you need to drill a bunch of holes at the same
depth, make your measurement, and then measure your
drill bit. Cut a piece of cork so it spans the difference,
slip it into a vice to hold it steady, and drill straight
down through the cork. Leave the cork on the bit and
you have a **handy depth-measuring guide.**

Cornstarch

This pantry staple is useful in every household.

HOME CARE & REPAIR

➤ If you need to fill some nail holes and find yourself out of putty, mix together cornstarch and water to make a nice smooth paste. Use that paste to **fill your nail holes.** It will work just as well as the putty. You can also use gritty toothpaste for a quick fill.

HOUSEKEEPING

➤ An easy way to **make your carpets cleaner** is to sprinkle the entire area with cornstarch about half an hour before you vacuum. After you vacuum, the carpet will look bright and clean.

➤ After cleaning wood furniture, sprinkle a little cornstarch over the area and rub with a lint-free cloth. It will **absorb excess polish and clean away fingerprints.**

STAIN REMOVAL

➤ **Remove greasy stains, such as lotions and baby oil, from clothing.** Blot as much as you can with a cloth; then sprinkle with some cornstarch. Let it sit for 10 minutes, shake it out, and dab with white vinegar to break up the grease. Then launder.

➤ **Remove a grease stain on leather** by sprinkling the spot with some cornstarch and letting it sit overnight. Brush it away in the morning—the cornstarch should have absorbed the grease.

PERSONAL CARE

If your shoes have gotten stinky, sprinkle some cornstarch inside at night to **absorb odors** by morning.

Cotton Balls

If you've ever wondered how anyone could use all the cotton balls in those gigantic bags, I have some ideas for you.

IN THE KITCHEN

➤ Soak some cotton balls with vanilla and put them in a dish in your refrigerator to **help absorb odors.**

HOUSEKEEPING

➤ Cotton balls can help you **clean hard-to-reach areas.** Soak cotton balls with bleach or other cleansers and stuff them into tight corners or other areas. Let them sit for a little while. Remove the cotton balls and rinse the areas clean.

➤ When you're ready to bring your Christmas tree inside, make a fresh cut straight across the trunk, then drill a hole in the bottom as far up as you can into the trunk. Stuff the hole with some cotton balls. The cotton will act as a wick and **help pull water up into the tree.**

➤ Soak a cotton ball with some wintergreen oil (available at most health food stores) and wipe it over the inside and under parts of musty antique furniture. The wintergreen oil will linger and **make the furniture smell fresher.**

➤ Use cotton balls to **bait a mousetrap.** Mice like it to line their nests, so it attracts them to the trap.

Cotton Swabs

These little beauties are great for getting into tight places.

IN THE WORKSHOP
➤ Cotton swabs are a great **tool in the workshop to apply glue, clean tools, oil parts, and touch up paint jobs.**

HOUSEKEEPING
➤ Keep cotton swabs as part of your laundry room tool kit for gently **applying your pretreaters to stains.**

➤ Use a cotton swab dipped in nail polish remover to **separate fingers stuck together by instant bonding glue.** The swab can be pushed and twisted easily between your fingers to get the remover right where you need it!

➤ **Remove dirt from the corners of a glass-front cabinet.** Grab a cotton swab and dip it in your cleanser. The swab is small enough to get rid of all that dirt.

Crayons

The colors and waxy base make crayons useful for more than just the kids' coloring projects.

HOME CARE & REPAIR

➤ Use an appropriate color crayon to **cover scratches and dents on wood furniture.** Simply soften the tip of the crayon with a hair dryer, rub it over the mark, and then buff it to a shine! Crayons will also **cover scratches and dings in vinyl floors**.

➤ Use a crayon to **cover the scratches on your kitchen appliances.**

KID STUFF

➤ **Give away small bundles of crayons, stickers, pencils, and even small toys as Halloween treats** so parents don't have to worry about unsafe treats.

HOUSEKEEPING

➤ Melt down crayons and use them to **make brightly colored candles.**

Mrs. Fixit's AMAZING!

If you find yourself with crayon marks on your walls, rub some toothpaste into the marks and they will disappear in no time! You can also clean them off with a damp cloth dipped in baking soda.

Housekeeping Tip

A B C D E F G H I J K L M N O P Q R S T U V W X Y Z

Cream of Tartar

STAIN REMOVAL

➤ **Remove stains from aluminum pans.** Mix 2 tablespoons of cream of tartar into a quart of water. Bring it to a boil, let it cool, and then scrub away the stains.

➤ Mix cream of tartar and water to form a paste, that will **get rid of lime scale.** It will also help **treat ring-around-the-collar stains.**

➤ **Eliminate rust stains on clothes.** If the clothes can take hot water, add a tablespoon of cream of tartar to a quart of boiling water. Boil the item for about 10 minutes and the stain should be gone. Another method is to treat the stain with a mixture of lemon juice and salt. Let it sit for a while, wash in hot water, and then lay it in the sun to dry.

➤ **Remove stains on marble or porcelain** by mixing together 3 parts cream of tartar to 1 part hydrogen peroxide. Spread the mixture over the stain, and let it dry thoroughly. Then you can just wipe it away with a soft cloth and some hot water.

IN THE KITCHEN

➤ Try this **substitute for buttermilk:** Stir together 1 cup of milk and $1^3/_4$ tablespoons cream of tartar.

➤ To **unclog a salt shaker,** use a toothpick to poke through the holes, then soak the lid in a small pot of boiling water and a teaspoon of cream of tartar to release the salt buildup.

Denture Tablets

Even if you don't wear dentures, keep a box of these tablets in the house to scour and shine all sorts of surfaces!

HOME CARE & REPAIR

➤ Drop a couple of tablets into a slow drain and run some hot water to **quickly clear the drain.**

➤ Denture tabs are an easy way to **clean the toilet.** Drop a couple of tablets into the bowl, let them fizz, and then flush for a pristine potty.

PERSONAL CARE

➤ Use a couple of tablets to **clean your favorite jewelry.** Put a tablet in a glass of water and drop in your diamonds or other jewelry. Leave them for a few minutes, then rinse. The gems will sparkle.

➤ Denture tabs can also be used to **clean toothbrushes.** Think about it: They are designed to kill bacteria on dentures so they can clean and disinfect toothbrushes too.

STAIN REMOVAL

➤ Use denture tablets to **remove hard-water stains from glassware and coffee decanters.** Match the amount of water to the right number of tabs per the instructions on the box, soak the item for a few minutes, and rinse clean.

➤ **Remove flower scum and deposits from your narrow-neck vases.** Fill a vase with water and drop in a tablet. When the fizzing has stopped, all of the scum and deposits will be gone.

Diapers

Whether you choose cloth diapers
or disposable diapers, put them to
use around the house.

IN THE WORKSHOP

➤ Cloth diapers are great to have in the workshop: My
favorite use—staining. Use absorbent diapers to **give
your furniture an even finish every time you stain.**

HOUSEKEEPING

➤ **Stock your home-cleaning kit** with cloth diapers.
For $10 to $15 for a package of 12, you get cleaning
cloths that are soft so they won't damage surfaces,
white so they won't transfer dyes, and wonderfully
washable so they last for years.

➤ Use a disposable diaper for **drainage when potting
plants.** Cut out a circle from a disposable diaper the
size of the bottom of your pot. Stick the diaper in, and
finish potting the plant. Now, when you water, the diaper
will absorb water and soil that otherwise might leak all
over your table. Plus, the gel crystals inside the diaper
will store the water so you won't need to water your
plants as often.

➤ This same concept will work for your Christmas tree.
Slit open a diaper and stuff the filling into your
Christmas tree stand; the crystals will soak up the
water and **feed the Christmas tree** as it needs it!

Dish Soap

Regular liquid dish soap gets the job done—and then some! Here are some quick and easy ways to put liquid soap to work around the house.

HOUSEKEEPING

➤ Dish soap **makes a great window cleaner.** Mix 1 teaspoon liquid dish soap and 1 teaspoon cornstarch in 1 gallon of water. Wipe it on with a sponge and squeegee it off. This mixture leaves windows and mirrors with a streak-free shine every time.

HOME CARE & REPAIR

➤ Use liquid dish soap to **find a tiny hole in your inflatable mattress.** Dip a washcloth into water mixed with a little dish soap. Wipe the cloth over the mattress and look for tiny bubbles. The escaping air creates soap bubbles so you can locate the hole and patch it.

IN THE KITCHEN

➤ To **remove stains in the microwave,** pour 1 cup of water into a microwave-safe bowl and add 1 tablespoon of white vinegar and a few drops of dish soap. Run the microwave on high for 5 minutes, then let sit for 10 more minutes. When the time is up, wipe away stains and buildup!

IN THE GARDEN

➤ **Get rid of pests that have been munching on plant leaves** by adding a few drops of dish soap to a spray bottle of room-temperature water, and spraying the plants each week with the mixture. Bugs don't like the soap and will leave the protected plant leaves alone.

Mrs. Fixit's AMAZING!

To keep a mirror fog-free, rub a few drops of liquid dish soap or a dollop of shaving cream onto the glass until it disappears. It will keep the mirror fog-free for up to two weeks! (This tip also works on eyeglasses and ski goggles.)

Housekeeping Tip

A B C D E F G H I J K L M N O P Q R S T U V W X Y Z

Dishwasher Detergent

Powdered automatic dishwasher detergent is an indispensable cleanser—even if you don't have a dishwasher!

HOME CARE & REPAIR

➤ Mix $\frac{1}{4}$ cup of detergent in 1 gallon of hot water to **make the perfect cleanser for painted walls and woodwork.**

> **TIP:** *Remember when you're washing walls, work from the bottom up so you don't get streaks!*

STAIN REMOVAL

➤ A little detergent on a damp sponge will **clean crayon and pencil marks off walls** too!

➤ A box in the bathroom will help you **cut through tough grout, hard-water or soap scum stains in tubs and showers easily.** It also puts a nice shine on your sinks and toilet bowls: Just sprinkle some detergent in the bowl and let it sit for a few minutes. Then scrub away the stains.

➤ Keep some handy to use for **stain removal in the laundry room.** Wet a stain, dab some dishwasher detergent onto it, and launder as usual.

Mrs. Fixit's AMAZING!

To whiten whites in the laundry, mix $\frac{1}{2}$ cup detergent into 1 gallon of hot water and soak overnight. Then wash in hot water.

Laundry Tip

Dryer Sheets

Don't throw away used dryer sheets! Stockpile them to use all over your house.

IN THE KITCHEN
➤ To **clean a particularly grimy pan,** put an unused dryer sheet inside the pan and fill with boiling water. Let it soak overnight. In the morning you'll be able to wash the pan clean without scouring.

HOME CARE & REPAIR
➤ Try used dryer sheets for **dusting jobs all over the house.** From televisions to tabletops, they'll pick up dust and eliminate the static that attracts it.

HOUSEKEEPING
➤ Dryer sheets **make great deodorizers.** Stick new or used sheets in sneakers, gym bags, and diaper pails.

➤ For **all-over-the-house freshness,** place a couple of new or used sheets in the vacuum-cleaner bag.

➤ **Make musty, dusty books smell fresh.** Put a couple of used sheets between the pages, and seal the book in a freezer bag for a few days.

IN THE GARAGE
➤ Keep a few new or used dryer sheets under car seats for **no-hassle freshening.**

STAIN REMOVAL
➤ **Eliminate water spots on mirrors and fixtures.** A quick swipe with a used dryer sheet will have everything from chrome to glass shining in no time.

Egg Cartons

Rather than recycle egg cartons, keep a couple for reuse around the house.

HOME CARE & REPAIR

➤ If you can feel a draft every time you walk by an outlet, don't get frustrated; fix it. Use the outlet cover as a template to cut a part of the top of a foam egg carton as an **insulation shell for the outlet.** No more drafts, and you've saved yourself some money.

HOUSEKEEPING

➤ **Store small fragile holiday ornaments in egg cartons.** They have individual compartments, they stack easily on top of each other, and they were made to cushion fragile items.

➤ This same tactic will also work to **organize your jewelry, small crafting items, or even fasteners in the workshop.**

➤ Use egg cartons as **cushioning material for shipping packages.**

IN THE GARDEN

➤ When you go to plant your seeds, there is no reason to buy expensive containers. Use an egg carton to **start seedlings.**

Mrs. Fixit's
AMAZING!

To keep tall boots shapely, stand an egg carton up in each boot before you stash them in the closet.

Personal Care Tip

Emery Boards

You probably have an emery board or two around your home. Don't just leave them at the bottom of the drawer—dig 'em out and put them to good use!

IN THE WORKSHOP

➤ An emery board is essentially sandpaper on a stick, so use it when you need to **sand little crevices and tight spots**—one side for the rough work and the other side for a smooth finish.

➤ Use an emery board to **sharpen your carpenter's pencils,** or any pencil in a pinch.

➤ Emery boards also work great to **clean wood sap or dried glue off the face of your hammer** when you're finished with a project.

HOME CARE & REPAIR

➤ Wet the fine side of an emery board and **smooth away small chips on glassware.**

STAIN REMOVAL

➤ **Remove stains on suede** by gently rubbing the stain with the fine side of an emery board. This will remove the stain and refresh the nap.

Food Coloring

Use food coloring to brighten up home projects.

HOME CARE & REPAIR

➤ To help you **find the leak in your toilet,** take the top off of the tank and put a few drops of food coloring in the water. Leave a note on the toilet so no one uses it, and wait an hour or two. Check to see where the food coloring ended up. If it found its way into the bowl, your flapper valve is leaking and probably needs to be replaced. Before you replace it, try lifting the flapper and scrubbing the inside seat. There may be some mineral deposits preventing you from getting a tight seal. If the colored water is dripping out the back of the toilet by the pipes, you need to replace the seal between the tank and the bowl. Still haven't found the problem? Flush the toilet. If the water pools up at the base of the toilet, the wax ring is cracked and needs to be replaced.

KID STUFF

➤ For a fun project with kids, **change the color of flowers with food coloring.** Add a few drops to a glass of water, put some white flowers in the glass and leave it overnight. In the morning the flowers will have absorbed the color like magic.

➤ To **make safe finger paints for kids**, use food coloring to tint plain yogurt. (Don't use this idea if your child is allergic to dairy products.)

Garbage Cans

They're tall, they're sturdy,
and they're a big help around
the house. With these ideas, you
might even run out to buy a few more.

IN THE GARDEN

➤ Use a big plastic garbage can on wheels as a **caddie
to eliminate extra trips to grab tools while
gardening.** Weight down the base with some bricks, a
bag of topsoil, or something else so that the can doesn't
tip over. Fill it with tools and then wheel it around the
yard with ease.

HOUSEKEEPING

➤ You can **organize all of your various rolls of
wrapping paper with a tall kitchen garbage can.**
Simply stand all of your rolls of paper on end in the
garbage can. This will keep them organized, and they
won't get squashed.

➤ **Store off-season clothes** in shorter round garbage
cans, then cover with a circle of plywood and drape with
a tablecloth for a small table. Great storage and an
extra piece of furniture in one!

KID STUFF

➤ You can also use garbage cans to **organize kids'
toys in the playroom or sports equipment in the
garage.** Buy a different color can for each category or
kid, and line them up against a wall for a neat and
inexpensive storage solution.

A B C D E F G H I J K L M N O P Q R S T U V W X Y Z

Garden Hose

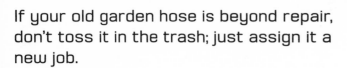

If your old garden hose is beyond repair, don't toss it in the trash; just assign it a new job.

IN THE GARDEN
➤ **Turn your leaky hose into a sprinkler.** Simply punch holes along the length of the hose and use it in the garden.

HOME CARE & REPAIR
➤ Use a piece of an old garden hose to **carry something with sharp edges,** such as a pane of glass. Slit the garden hose lengthwise and slip it over the ends of the glass. Now you have a cushion for your hands.

IN THE WORKSHOP
➤ **Protect your saw blades** by cutting a slit along a length of garden hose and slipping it over your saw blades. It will protect you and them.

KID STUFF
➤ If the chains on your backyard swing set are too sharp for little fingers, slip a length of garden hose over the chain to **protect kids' hands while they swing.**

Mrs. Fixit's

AMAZING!

Spring a leak? Pick up a hose coupler for a quick and easy repair.

Yard Care Tip

A B C D E F G H I J K L M N O P Q R S T U V W X Y Z

Golf Tees

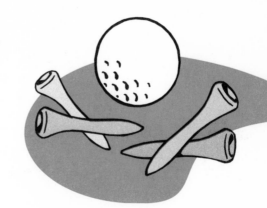

"Fore" holes, hinges, and helping! Grab your extra golf tees for these handy uses.

HOME CARE & REPAIR

➤ **Tighten a loose screw** by taking it out and filling the hole with an old golf tee. Cut the tee off flush and twist the screw back into place. The golf tee will help it hold fast!

➤ **Take care of loose door hinges.** Fill all of the holes with golf tees. Gently tap them in place with a hammer, cut them flush, and remount the door. The tees are stronger filler than putty.

IN THE WORKSHOP

➤ If you're doing a woodworking project, **fill recessed screw holes with natural wood golf tees.** Cut off the bottom, tap the top of the tee into the hole, and sand flush for a neat and tidy appearance.

HOUSEKEEPING

➤ **Make a simple tie rack.** Get a length of 1x2 and drill holes in a zigzag pattern along the length. Tap the tees into place, paint, and you'll have a unique tie rack at very little cost.

Gum

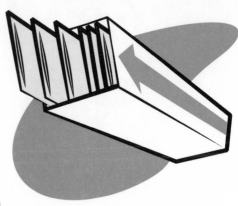

Pick up an extra pack of chewing gum next time you're at the grocery store. Try it for these unique uses.

IN THE KITCHEN

➤ **Prevent mealworms from getting into the dry foods** you keep in your cupboards. Put a stick or two of spearmint gum on the shelves where you store these foods. Mealworms don't like the mint and will stay out.

➤ You can also **set a piece of spearmint gum on your plate at a picnic to keep flies away** from your food.

➤ You'll **tear up less** if you chew a stick of gum the next time you're peeling onions.

HOME CARE & REPAIR

➤ **Retrieve something you've dropped down a heating grate** by chewing a big wad of bubble gum. Stick it to the end of a wire coat hanger (unwind the hanger first) and lower the hanger into the grate. Stick the gum to the item and slowly pull it back up.

IN THE GARDEN

➤ Do you have a mole hole in your yard? **Chase moles away** by slipping a few pieces of spearmint gum into the hole. Moles will burrow the other way!

Mrs. Fixit's

AMAZING!

PESTS BE GONE!
Mix 3 tablespoons of peppermint soap, which can be found in health food stores, in a spray bottle with 12 to 16 ounces of water. Then spritz it around openings and pipes to keep mice and squirrels from trying to enter the house.
As a bonus, ants hate peppermint too, so you can take care of three pests with one squirt!

Home Care Tip

Hair Dryer

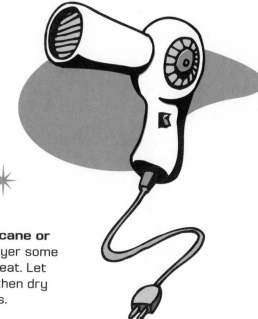

Use the heat-producing quality of your hair dryer to warm up to these household projects.

HOUSEKEEPING

➤ You can easily **fix the seat of a sagging cane or rush chair.** Turn the chair upside down and layer some steaming hot towels over the bottom of the seat. Let the towels stay there for a few minutes and then dry with a hair dryer; this should tighten the reeds.

➤ **Remove wax on the wall** by aiming a hot hair dryer at the wax for a minute and then carefully scraping it away with a credit card. Follow up with a cloth dipped in white vinegar to remove any waxy residue.

➤ Aim a hair dryer at a bumper sticker, a vinyl tile, or a bathtub decal to **loosen the glue and make removal easier.**

➤ If you have some old magnetic photo albums, the pages can yellow and deteriorate over time, which can harm your photos. The easiest way to **remove photos from a photo album** without damaging them is to set your hair dryer on low and carefully aim it at the side of the album (not directly on the pictures). As the page heats slightly, you will be able to slowly peel up the picture.

IN THE BATH

➤ One of the biggest problems with the bathroom mirror is that it gets all fogged up. To quickly **defog your mirror**, aim your hair dryer at the glass. The dry heat will clear the fog.

Hair Spray

You can do more than keep your style in shape with hair spray!

STAIN REMOVAL

➤ Use hair spray to **remove ink and marker stains from clothes, carpets, linens, and even skin**. Simply spray a good amount on the stain, let it set for a minute, and then wash the item.

KID STUFF

➤ **Preserve pictures your child has drawn using chalk or pencil** with a gentle spray over the surface. The hair spray seals the surface so the picture won't get smudged and ruined.

HOUSEKEEPING

➤ **Protect newspaper articles from smudging** with a gentle coating of hair spray. This is a short-term solution, however; don't do this if you want to save the article for a long time—it will yellow. (Laminate the article if you want it to last longer.)

➤ **Preserve a dried-flower arrangement** with hair spray. This will also keep dust from clinging to it.

➤ You will also want to **preserve the arrangement's decorative ribbons** to help keep them clean. Spray the bows lightly to stiffen the ribbon.

Mrs. Fixit's **AMAZING!**

Slow down an annoying flying insect by spritzing it with a little hair spray as it flies by. The spray freezes its wings so you can easily catch it.

Home Care Tip

Hydrogen Peroxide

If you think hydrogen peroxide is useful only in the first-aid department, think again.

STAIN REMOVAL

➤ **Remove stains on marble or porcelain** by mixing 3 parts cream of tartar to 1 part hydrogen peroxide. Spread the mixture over the stain and let it dry thoroughly. Then you can just wipe it away with a soft cloth and some hot water.

➤ Use hydrogen peroxide to **remove blood and other protein-based stains from clothing.** Dab some peroxide into the spot with a cotton swab, and then launder as usual. It will also help remove scorch marks from cotton fabrics.

IN THE BATH

➤ Use hydrogen peroxide to **kill mold and mildew spores on bathroom surfaces.**

➤ **Remove leftover sticker goo on your bathtub.** Mix cream of tartar and hydrogen peroxide together to form a thick paste. Use that paste to scrub the stains. They'll clean away, and the tub will shine like new.

HOUSEKEEPING

➤ **Preserve fresh flowers.** When arranging flowers, fill your vase with cool—not cold—water, add a teaspoon of hydrogen peroxide, and then arrange the flowers in your vase.

Ice

Keep those ice-cube trays full, ready to solve a few household dilemmas.

IN THE KITCHEN

➤ **Safeguard your family from eating spoiled food** in the event of a power outage while you're out of town. The food in your freezer can defrost and refreeze without your knowledge. If you cook that food, you and your family can become ill. Keep a small container of ice cubes in the freezer. If you come back and the cubes appear to have melted, you'll know the freezer was off and to throw everything away!

➤ When you're done making lemonade, don't throw away the lemon rinds; toss them in the garbage disposal with a couple of ice cubes. This will **keep your garbage disposal blades clean and smelling sweet.**

➤ **Clean your blender** by throwing a handful of ice cubes and some lukewarm soapy water into it. Turn it on and let it run on high for a couple of minutes. The ice scours the blades and can get all of the hard-to-reach areas nice and clean.

HOUSEKEEPING

➤ **Bring carpet back to its original fullness** by placing an ice cube or two on crushed areas. As the ice melts the moisture will plump up the carpet fibers. Once the ice has completely melted, use a towel to brush the carpet fibers back to their original shape.

➤ **Remove gum in hair and on clothing** with ice. Hold some ice over the gum until it is nice and stiff, then chip it away.

Kitty Litter

The absorbent qualities of kitty litter can help clean and deodorize around the house.

IN THE KITCHEN

➤ **Protect your kitchen garbage can from odors and leaks.** Sprinkle some kitty litter in the bottom of your garbage can. It will help absorb odors, and it will catch drips if the bag leaks so you have less of a mess to clean up later.

HOUSEKEEPING

➤ To **properly dispose of latex paint,** you need to allow it to harden. To speed up the process, pour some kitty litter into it. Once the paint hardens, you can throw it out with the regular garbage.

➤ **Absorb excess moisture and odors in your basement and workshop.** Sprinkle kitty litter in coffee cans and place them strategically around the area.

STAIN REMOVAL

➤ **Clean up oil or grease spills on concrete** by immediately spreading kitty litter over the stain. Allow it to sit for several hours; then just sweep away the litter and the stain.

Lemonade Mix

Citric acid is a great cleanser—and you probably have some of this miracle ingredient in your home. It's in powdered lemonade mix!

HOME CARE & REPAIR

➤ **Clear up a clogged showerhead** by dissolving a scoop of lemonade mix in hot water and soaking the fixture overnight to loosen and remove mineral buildup.

➤ **Shine dingy toilets** with a scoop of lemonade mix. Pour the lemonade mix into the bowl and let it soak for 15 minutes. Then just swish and flush.

IN THE KITCHEN

➤ That same citric acid will also **clean the inside of your dishwasher.** Fill the soap cup and run the machine through a cycle with no dishes. It will clean the racks, the jets, and the walls with ease.

➤ Use lemonade mix to **remove berry stains and garlic odors from your hands.** Wet your hands, rub in a small scoop of lemonade mix, and scrub. The gritty powder scrubs your hands clean, and the citric acid removes stains and odors from your skin.

STAIN REMOVAL

➤ Lemonade mix also comes in handy to **remove stains on clothes** in the laundry room. Make it into a paste with some cool water, and spread the paste over stains such as coffee, tea, red wine, and rust. Just remember to test your clothes for colorfastness before you try this or you could bleach the spot.

Lemons & Lemon Juice

If lemons automatically make you think fresh and clean, put them to work for just that purpose.

HOUSEKEEPING

➤ To **clean copper,** cut a fresh lemon in half, dip it in some salt, and scrub. The tarnish and gunk will literally disappear before your eyes; then simply wash in warm, soapy water.

➤ To **remove water spots on your crystal,** just rub them with a soft cloth that has been dipped in lemon juice. Those spots will be gone in no time.

➤ **Clean and disinfect switchplates** with a quick wipe using a cloth dipped in lemon juice. This will clean them up in a jiff! This trick also works well on doorknobs and refrigerator door handles.

IN THE KITCHEN

➤ If you only need a little **lemon juice for a recipe,** pierce the skin of the lemon with a toothpick and squeeze out the amount you need.

IN THE BATH

➤ Bathroom sinks can end up with buildup and deposits—this is called lime scale and it shows up when you have hard water. To **eliminate lime scale,** cut a lemon in half and use it to scrub the area—this will cut through the scaling.

Mrs. Fixit's
AMAZING!

Making lemonade? Get the most juice out of your lemons by microwaving them for 5 to 8 seconds before you juice them.

Kitchen Tip

Lip
Balm

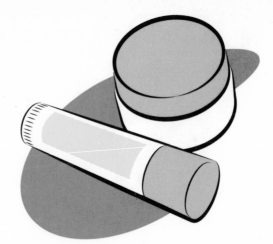

Use the lubricating quality of lip balm for projects around the house.

HOME CARE & REPAIR

➤ Keep some lip balm with you when you're working with screws. Believe it or not, **rubbing it over the end of a screw will make driving it a lot easier.**

➤ Use lip balm to **silence squeaky doors.** Simply pull out the hinge pin, coat it with lip balm, and tap it back into place.

PERSONAL CARE

➤ Coat a **sticky zipper** with a little lip balm.

➤ Use a little lip balm to **soothe the pain of a paper cut** and stop the bleeding. The same concept applies if you **nick yourself shaving.**

Liquid Fabric Softener

You can soften more than laundry with liquid fabric softener.

HOME CARE & REPAIR

➤ To **remove wallpaper,** mix ¼ cup liquid fabric softener into 1 gallon of hot water in a 5-gallon bucket. Put a paint grid over the side. First, use a scoring tool to perforate the paper. Next, use a paint roller to spread the mixture over the walls. Let it sit for a few minutes, and then simply scrape off the wallpaper. When the paper is removed, reapply the solution to remove paste residue. A window squeegee can make quick work of this job.

➤ **Keep the bristles of your paintbrush soft**. When you're finished cleaning your paintbrushes, give them a final rinse in 1 gallon hot water and 2 tablespoons of liquid fabric softener.

HOUSEKEEPING

➤ To **keep vinyl floors shiny,** damp-mop every once in a while with ½ cup liquid fabric softener in 1 gallon of warm water.

➤ To **clean glass tabletops,** mix together 2 teaspoons liquid fabric softener and 1 pint warm water. Spray this solution on and wipe it down with a soft lint-free cloth.

➤ **Prevent static electricity that attracts dirt to carpets.** Once a week, mix together 1¼ cups of water with ¼ cup of fabric softener. Lightly spray the carpet with that solution—you should have a lot less dirt.

Magnets

You'll find plenty
of "attractive" ways to use
magnets to help around the house.

IN THE WORKSHOP

➤ Glue a magnet to the bottom of your hammer. This
way you can stick the handle into the can of nails
and easily **grab a few nails.**

➤ Attach a magnetic strip to the side of your hammer
to **keep track of tiny nails** while you're working.

HOME CARE & REPAIR

➤ To **retrieve a bunch of little nails, pins, or paper
clips,** try this: Grab a plastic deli container and a heavy-
duty magnet. Pull the lid off of the container and hold
the magnet on top of the lid. Then hover over the spilled
items. When you've grabbed a bunch, put the lid on the
container and pull the magnet away. Picked up and put
away with minimal effort!

IN THE BATH

➤ If tweezers and clippers are cluttering the bottom of
the medicine cabinet, attach some magnets to the
inside of the door. You can easily **hang small metal
tools** out of the way.

➤ A magnet tied to a string will **fish clippers,
tweezers, and bobby pins out of a sink drain.**

Mayonnaise

More than a condiment, mayonnaise is the solution to some common household problems.

HOME CARE & REPAIR

➤ Mayo is a great cleaner and conditioner for wood furniture. **Revitalize a dried wood surface** by just spreading some mayonnaise over the surface and working it in with a soft cloth. Leave the coating on for a few minutes, then wipe away the excess with a clean cloth. The piece will look like new.

➤ Use mayo to **take white water rings off wood.** Spread it over the affected area, and wipe it off. For a deep-set ring, you may have to let the mayo soak into the spot overnight.

IN THE GARAGE

➤ **Remove tree sap from your car** by rubbing mayo into the area and allowing it to sit for a few minutes; mayo softens the sap so you can easily clean it away.

➤ Mayo's softening power will also **loosen tar from your car.**

HOUSEKEEPING

➤ If your child drew on your wood furniture with crayons, rub a little bit of mayonnaise into the spot with a soft cloth. It will **lift crayon marks** in no time.

➤ **Remove price stickers stuck to glass** by spreading mayonnaise over the sticker and letting it sit for a few minutes. The mayo releases the glue's grip, and you can wipe away the sticker with ease.

Mrs. Fixit's
AMAZING!

An old mayonnaise jar is a perfect hiding place for valuables. Pour some white paint inside and swirl it around to coat the entire surface. Let it dry completely and store your valuables in it. Then put it on a shelf in the cupboard or the back of the refrigerator.

Safekeeping Tip

A B C D E F G H I J K L **M** N O P Q R S T U V W X Y Z

Milk Jugs

Rinse out those old milk jugs and cartons, and put them to good use.

IN THE GARDEN

➤ Use pint-size cartons—or full-size cartons cut down to size—to **start seedlings** before the spring planting season.

➤ Punch some holes in the bottom of a gallon-size milk jug and fill it full of grass seed. It's a great way to **seed the lawn.**

> TIP: *In cold weather, punch holes in the bottom of a plastic milk jug and fill it with sand or rock salt to sprinkle on driveways and walkways to get rid of ice.*

HOME CARE & REPAIR

➤ Use milk jug totes as a **clothespin caddie or as a handheld bucket for small painting projects.**

➤ Cut off the entire top of a jug and make a **waterproof storage container** for steel wool pads and sponges under your sink.

IN THE WORKSHOP

➤ Recycle plastic jugs by cutting an opening in the side, keeping the handle intact to **make a tote for small tools, screws, and nails.**

➤ Line up several milk jug totes for **storage in your workroom.**

> TIP: *Cut the tops off of several cartons and use them to organize socks, stockings, and jewelry in dresser drawers. Or use them to protect small items when you're moving. Just slip your knickknacks inside and you don't have to worry about them getting damaged.*

Money Matters

Follow these spare tips for spare change—and really make your money work for you!

HOME CARE & REPAIR

➤ Use a quarter to **open a paint can**. It's the perfect thickness, it's a handy size to grip, and you won't damage the can.

➤ A dime is thin enough to **tighten screws.** Slip it in the slot and tighten away!

➤ A penny can **prevent corrosion on your car battery.** Place a penny by the terminals and corrosion will gather on the penny, not the battery.

➤ Any coins will come in handy to **fix a wobbly table.** Either slip a coin or two under a foot on the table or wedge it into the joint that's causing the wobble in the first place.

➤ Spare change can help you **sew a button** too. Place the coin on the underside of the fabric and line it up with the holes on your button. This will give you a handy guide so that you can easily find the holes in the button and you won't prick your fingers.

➤ Fill an old bottle or decorative tin with coins to **make a doorstop or bookend.**

Mrs. Fixit's AMAZING!

Bills can work hard around the house, too. A dollar bill is just over six inches long, making it a handy measuring device in a pinch.

Home Care Tip

Nail Polish Remover

You'll find this savvy solution does more than make the most of a manicure.

STAIN REMOVAL

➤ If your little one made a mess with a marker, reach for the remover. Just a little on a cloth **removes marker and ink** from appliances, glass, stainless steel—and your skin! Be sure to clean the area and your hands with soapy water when you're done.

➤ **Eliminate scuff marks** on vinyl and tile floors as well as white leather shoes with a dab of nail polish remover.

HOME CARE & REPAIR

➤ **Buff off messy sticker residue** on the glass in picture frames with some nail polish remover on a cotton ball or soft cloth.

➤ **Loosen the grip of superglue** that left fingers stuck together. Use a cotton swab dipped in remover to gently work the fingers apart.

➤ **Clean up bread bag residue** melted on the top of the toaster oven. Once it's cool, use an old washcloth with nail polish remover.

➤ If your manicure went awry, use the remover to **get nail polish out of cotton fabrics**. First, test for colorfastness, treat the stains with a dab of remover, and then wash the clothes in cold water.

➤ Nail polish remover is also great to **remove tar and paint from cotton fabric.**

Nylons

Don't ditch those nylons
with runs—keep a stash
of them for household projects.

HOUSEKEEPING

➤ To **clean window screens** without taking
them off, wipe them every couple of weeks with
an old pair of nylon stockings. They will scrub
off dust without damaging your screens.

➤ Slip the leg of an old pair of nylons over a yardstick
to **lift cobwebs from high corners** and **clean under
the fridge and stove.**

Secure a stocking over the outlet hose on your washing
machine to **collect lint.**

IN THE WORKSHOP

➤ Use nylons to **check the smoothness of your
finish when woodworking.** Run a stocking across the
surface. The nylon will snag rough spots.

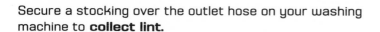

➤ Nylons are great to **apply stain to unfinished
wood** because they don't absorb too much of the
stain and it goes on nice and even.

HOME CARE & REPAIR

➤ If you're using old paint, you may want to **strain the
paint to get rid of lumps.** An easy way is to stretch
an old pair of nylon stockings over the top of a
container. Use rubber bands to secure it and pour paint
through the stocking. As the paint goes through the
nylon mesh, lumps will get caught.

IN THE YARD

➤ Slip the leg of a nylon stocking over the end of the
downspout as you **clean the gutters.** As debris is
flushed down, it won't make a mess in the yard.

Olive Oil

Olive oil is used in hundreds of recipes, but did you know it can be used for many other household tasks?

HOME CARE & REPAIR
➤ **Repair dented and pitted wood furniture** by rubbing a little olive oil over the damaged surface. The dents will blend in with the rest of the finish.

IN THE GARDEN
➤ In the yard olive oil can help **keep moles away.** Saturate an old rag with olive oil and stuff it into a mole hole. The animals hate the smell and will stay far away.

HOUSEKEEPING
➤ Use olive oil to **shine plant leaves.** A little dab on a paper towel wiped over the leaves will make your plants look great.

➤ **Revitalize leather shoes or baseball gloves** with olive oil. Put a little on a soft cloth and work it into the leather. Just remember a little oil goes a long way.

➤ Olive oil is a great **cleaner for greasy, grimy hands.** Rub it in and wipe it away with a paper towel.

IN THE KITCHEN
➤ Olive oil is perfect for **seasoning cast-iron cookware, wooden cutting boards, and salad bowls.** Use the oil sparingly.

PERSONAL CARE
➤ **Restore dry hands and feet** by rubbing in olive oil at bedtime. Slip on a pair of cotton gloves and socks; your skin will be silky smooth by morning.

Onion Bags

Keep the mesh bags that onions
come in to help with household chores.

HOUSEKEEPING
➤ Onion bags make great **scrubbers for dishes,
windshields, bathtubs, and showers.**

➤ An onion bag filled with chalk will **absorb excess
moisture** if you hang it under your bathroom or
kitchen sink.

➤ Secure an onion bag over the end of your vacuum
hose when you vacuum around knickknacks. That will
**keep your treasures from being sucked into
the vacuum**.

IN THE KITCHEN
➤ Stuff some onion bags into the bottom of the
utensil basket in your dishwasher to **keep silverware
from slipping through and getting caught on
the racks.**

A B C D E F G H I J K L M N O P Q R S T U V W X Y Z

Oven Cleaner

A real workhorse, oven cleaner can really help out around the house. Just make sure you wear rubber gloves and have plenty of ventilation when using this product!

> **TIP:** *When using an oven cleaner, don't forget to follow the manufacturer's directions on the label.*

IN THE KITCHEN

➤ If no amount of scrubbing seems to **clean glass bakeware,** spray the piece outside with oven cleaner, put it in a plastic garbage bag, seal, and leave it for a couple of hours. Be careful of the fumes! Turn the bag away from your face when you open it outside, and remove the piece. Clean the bakeware well in dish soap and hot water several times to remove the cleaner and the spots.

HOME CARE & REPAIR

➤ Oven cleaner can easily **strip paint off metal and wood.** Spray it on, leave it for a couple of hours, and scrape away the paint.

➤ Oven cleaner also **removes soot and buildup from brick fireplaces.** Spray on the stained area, let it soak for 15 minutes, and then scrub away the stains. Rinse with plenty of warm water.

➤ If you have **grimy, dirty windows,** spritz them with some oven cleaner and wipe clean with a damp cloth.

Paintbrushes

Good for more than just applying paint and finishes, a paintbrush is a flexible household tool.

IN THE KITCHEN
➤ Use a new natural-bristle paintbrush for **basting, buttering and greasing everything from muffin tins to barbecue racks**—they're an indispensable tool and much cheaper than basting brushes.

KID STUFF
➤ Pack a paintbrush in your beach bag. It is a great tool for **brushing sand off** of your kids, toys, and even yourself.

HOUSEKEEPING
➤ Paintbrushes are great cleaning tools—the bristles **clean tight spaces and tiny spots** impossible to reach with a rag or sponge. Use them to dust lampshades, moldings, wicker, carved wood, and computer keyboards. The bristles are sturdy enough to clean cracks and crevices easily, and flexible enough not to damage delicate surfaces.

➤ Keep a paintbrush to **swish stain remover or liquid detergent over stains in the laundry room:** You'll waste less than you would by simply pouring these products onto spots.

Mrs. Fixit's

AMAZING!

Keep paintbrushes nice and soft by adding a drop of fabric softener to a bucket of rinse water every time you clean a brush!

Paint Tip

Paper Towels

There's no end in sight for ways to use paper towels. Here are a few ideas you might not have tried yet.

HOUSEKEEPING

➤ If you stack cast-iron pans in your cupboard, put paper towels between them. This will **absorb excess moisture in the cast-iron pans** and prevent rusting during storage.

➤ **Prevent chipping fine pieces of china** when you store them by placing paper towels between each piece.

➤ **Clean up spilled wax** on carpets, clothing, and linens by using a dry iron. Layer several paper towels over the wax, and slide a hot iron over the towels. The heat from the iron will transfer the wax to the towels— no muss, no fuss. If you're using an ironing board, protect the surface with a brown paper bag or more paper towels.

IN THE KITCHEN

➤ Are you looking for an easy way to **clean your stainless-steel sink?** Before you go to bed, soak some paper towels with diluted bleach and line the sink with them. When you get up in the morning, just rinse and the sink will shine.

➤ Use a paper towel as an easy **substitute for coffee filters.**

Paste Wax

For protecting plenty of household surfaces, paste wax does the trick.

HOME CARE & REPAIR

➤ **Eliminate condensation from the outside of a sweaty toilet.** Turn off the water and flush the toilet to drain the tank. Dry the inside, and apply a thin coat of the wax to the inside. This seals the tank's interior and prevents further condensation.

➤ **Seal the wood and protect furniture from drying out** by rubbing wax on the unfinished underside of each piece.

IN THE KITCHEN

➤ **Protect the metal racks in your refrigerator.** Apply paste wax to keep them from pitting and also help prevent rust and corrosion.

➤ **Shine the outside of your appliances** by rubbing paste wax on the outside. It will also help repel dust and fingerprints.

IN THE WORKSHOP

➤ Apply a thin coat of wax to **protect tools from rust and corrosion.**

Mrs. Fixit's

AMAZING!

To clean stainless-steel appliances before you wax them, rub gently with soap and water on a "0000" steel-wool pad. This will clean away grime and buff away imperfections. Then follow up with a thin coat of paste wax and buff to a shine.

Housekeeping Tip

A B C D E F G H I J K L M N O **P** Q R S T U V W X Y Z

Peanut Butter

Ooey, gooey peanut butter is actually a great household cleaner; here's how to put it to use.

HOUSEKEEPING

➤ Peanut butter will **remove sticker goo** from all sorts of items. Just rub it over the sticky mess, leave it for a few minutes, and then wipe away the gunk.

➤ This will also work to **remove black residue left on your skin by plastic bandages.**

➤ As a last resort, use peanut butter to **remove gum from fabric**. Rub it into the gum, let it sit for 15 minutes, and then scrape it away with the edge of a spoon. To remove the grease stain left by the peanut butter, treat with a good-quality dish soap or shampoo for oily hair.

KID STUFF

➤ **Clean ink marks off of toys** with peanut butter. It will take the ink off and you won't have to worry about your children putting the toy in their mouths. The "cleanser" won't hurt them.

Penetrating Oil

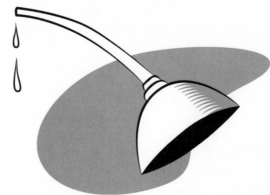

Having a few cans of this all-purpose product around the house will come in handy for all kinds of chores.

HOUSEKEEPING

➤ **Remove Silly Putty™** that's been matted into your carpet by spraying liberally with penetrating oil. Let it sit for a minute and then clean off as much as possible with a spoon. Clean the area with warm soapy water and white cloths to remove any traces of the oil and putty.

➤ Spray a little on tile floors to **remove scuff marks.** Spritz and swipe with a soft white cloth.

➤ **Eliminate crayon marks** from painted walls and woodwork. Spray penetrating oil and wipe with a white cloth to remove the marks in no time.

IN THE WORKSHOP

➤ **Coat your saw blade with a thin layer of penetrating oil to prevent rust** prior to storing. When you're done with a project, clean your saw so it doesn't get gummed up, brush off any sawdust, and wipe the blade with penetrating oil.

HOME CARE & REPAIR

➤ **Lubricate a nail** to make sure it goes in smoothly. To do this, simply store your nails in a jar with some penetrating oil.

IN THE GARDEN

➤ A light spray **keeps gardening tools rust free.**

Petroleum Jelly

This medicine cabinet staple seems to rarely get used—read this and you'll be reaching for it several times a week.

IN THE YARD

➤ **Keep garden tools from rusting** in storage by rubbing a thin coat of petroleum jelly on them.

➤ **Keep the squirrels out of your bird feeder.** Coat the pole with petroleum jelly. When the squirrels try to make their way up to the food they'll slip and get discouraged.

➤ **Prevent ants from getting into your dog's food** outside by simply putting a ring of petroleum jelly around the outside of the dish to keep the bugs out.

HOUSEKEEPING

➤ **Shine and protect patent leather shoes** with a little petroleum jelly.

➤ When you **assemble an artificial Christmas tree,** put a thin coat of petroleum jelly on the pieces of the trunk. You may also want to coat the ends of the branches, depending upon the type of tree you have. This will make it much easier to pull the tree apart at season's end.

➤ A thin coat on the base of a lightbulb before you put it in a lamp or fixture will **keep your bulb from getting stuck.** This works especially well on outdoor fixtures.

Pillowcases

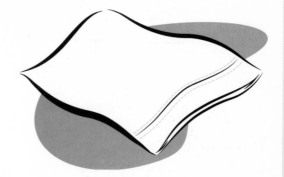

Past-their-prime pillowcases
can accumulate in no time.
But don't toss them out!
They have plenty of uses
all around the house.

HOUSEKEEPING
➤ Hang a pillowcase on the inside of your closet door
to **collect dirty laundry**.

HOME CARE & REPAIR
➤ You could also use them to **create a dustcover for
seldom-used clothes** in your closet. Just cut a small
hole in the top for a hanger and slip the clothes inside.

➤ **Keep seasonal decorations from getting dirty** by
making a dustcover out of an old pillowcase for small
Christmas trees, Easter baskets, and wreaths.

KID STUFF
➤ A pillowcase comes in handy on a baby's changing
table. Slip a pillowcase over the vinyl insert and **your
baby won't have to lie on cold vinyl.** A pillowcase is
easier to remove and wash than traditional covers.

➤ **Make an instant smock or apron** for your little
one by cutting holes for the head and arms into
an old pillowcase.

➤ In children's rooms, hang an old pillowcase
on the inside of the closet door to **corral stuffed
animals and toys.**

A
B
C
D
E
F
G
H
I
J
K
L
M
N
O
P
Q
R
S
T
U
V
W
X
Y
Z

Product Patrol

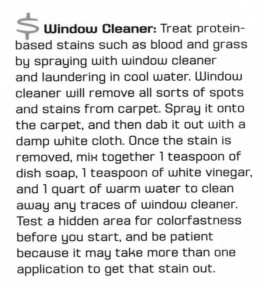

Product patrol here, saving you money. No need to buy that special item for each task. I have some products that will do double, triple, even quadruple duty!

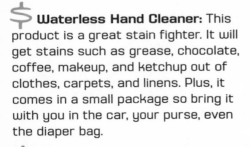

Waterless Hand Cleaner: This product is a great stain fighter. It will get stains such as grease, chocolate, coffee, makeup, and ketchup out of clothes, carpets, and linens. Plus, it comes in a small package so bring it with you in the car, your purse, even the diaper bag.

Plain White Toothpaste: It will shine your pearly grin, but its gentle abrasive also buffs away floor scratches, and removes white moisture rings from wood furniture. It will also shine a piece of tarnished silver and buff away that cloudy residue on glassware. How's that for a product that packs a punch!

Dishwasher Detergent: Mix a cup into a bucket of warm water and use it to clean painted woodwork and cabinetry. It also cleans soot off your fireplace. Don't forget to wear rubber gloves and rinse well.

Window Cleaner: Treat protein-based stains such as blood and grass by spraying with window cleaner and laundering in cool water. Window cleaner will remove all sorts of spots and stains from carpet. Spray it onto the carpet, and then dab it out with a damp white cloth. Once the stain is removed, mix together 1 teaspoon of dish soap, 1 teaspoon of white vinegar, and 1 quart of warm water to clean away any traces of window cleaner. Test a hidden area for colorfastness before you start, and be patient because it may take more than one application to get that stain out.

Rice

Sure rice is nice for dinner, but it can be used all through the day.

IN THE WORKSHOP
➤ Stick some rice in your toolbox to absorb moisture and **keep tools rust free.**

IN THE KITCHEN
➤ To **clean and sharpen the blades on your coffee grinder,** pour ½ cup of uncooked rice into the grinder and run it for a minute or so.

STAIN REMOVAL
➤ **Get rid of scale and scum in a narrow-neck vase** by pouring a small handful of rice and some white vinegar in the vase. Cover the top and shake those stains away.

HOUSEKEEPING
➤ Use rice to **weight the bottom of luminarias** to line your walkways during the holidays.

KID STUFF
➤ Fill a shallow plastic tote (like an under-bed storage box) with rice to **make a fun, indoor "sandbox"** for the kids. When they're not using it, pop the top back on and stick it on a shelf.

A B C D E F G H I J K L M N O P Q R S T U V W X Y Z

Rubber Gloves

The nonslip grip of rubber gloves gives you a great grasp on a lot of tasks throughout the house.

HOME CARE & REPAIR
➤ **Keep mops and brooms in place** by snipping the fingertips off an old pair of rubber gloves, and slipping them over the tops of the handles. When you lean the brooms against the wall, they'll stay secure and won't make marks.

➤ You can also slip the tips over chair feet to **protect the floors.**

IN THE WORKSHOP
➤ **Prevent pliers and wrenches from slipping or marring surfaces.** Slip rubber glove fingertips over the jaws.

HOUSEKEEPING
➤ Cut the cuffs off a rubber glove to **make a large-scale rubber band.**

PERSONAL CARE
➤ Fill a rubber glove with water, roll the cuff to hold in the water, and clip it closed with a bag clip. Stick the water-filled glove in the freezer to **create an inexpensive ice pack for sore muscles,** or toss it in the cooler on your next picnic to **keep food chilled.**

Mrs. Fixit's
AMAZING!

Before you pull on a pair of rubber gloves, coat your hands with your favorite hand cream. As you work, the heat and lotion work together to give you supersoft hands.

Personal Care Tip

Rubbing Alcohol

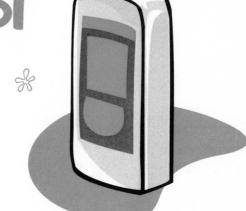

Rubbing alcohol is a great cleaner. It not only disinfects household surfaces but also leaves a streak-free shine.

PERSONAL CARE

➤ **Unclog your hair spray or spray paint nozzle** by gently pulling the spray top off and soaking it in rubbing alcohol for 10 minutes or so.

HOUSEKEEPING

➤ **Remove hair spray buildup on walls, floors, and mirrors** by dipping an old washcloth into some rubbing alcohol and wiping it away.

➤ **Wipe the dust off of decorative candles** by cleaning them with a cloth dipped in some rubbing alcohol. It takes off dust and dirt so your candles look like new. Be careful not to get rubbing alcohol on the wick.

IN THE GARAGE

➤ Use rubbing alcohol to **clean your windshield wiper blades.** It will cut easily through road grime and it discourages ice from forming on them.

IN THE GARDEN

➤ After you're through cutting back diseased plants in the garden, **wash your garden tools** in a solution of three parts rubbing alcohol and one part water. This will kill the germs so you won't infect your plants the next time you use the tools.

Mrs. Fixit's
AMAZING!

Rubbing alcohol is a great all-purpose cleaner for mirrors. It cleans, shines, and disinfects in one quick step!

Home Care Tip

Salt

It's a good idea to have plenty of salt on hand; you won't believe how it can help around your house.

IN THE KITCHEN

➤ **Keep your kitchen drain running smoothly** by pouring a strong solution of hot salt water (2 parts water to 1 part salt) down the drain every few weeks.

➤ Salt can **enhance your coffee's flavor and remove any bitter taste.** Put a pinch of salt in the filter with your coffee before you brew.

➤ **Clean discolored glassware** by soaking it in a solution of one part salt to eight parts of white vinegar.

HOUSEKEEPING

➤ **Create a base for arranging artificial flowers** by filling the bottom of the vase with salt to hold the stems in place. If you use kosher salt, the crystals add a nice decorative touch as well.

➤ **Prevent colors from bleeding in the laundry** by adding ¼ cup salt along with your detergent.

PERSONAL CARE

➤ Salt can **help nylon stockings last longer.** Mix 2 cups salt in 1 gallon of warm water. Soak the nylons for a few hours and rinse them in cold water several times.

Sand

The gritty nature of sand comes in handy for lots of household projects.

IN THE GARDEN

➤ The key to a beautiful container garden is the soil. **Mix your own potting soil** by combining two parts of peat moss with one part of builder's sand.

➤ When you're finished in the garden, **prevent rust on your garden tools.** Fill a 5-gallon paint bucket with sand. Add 1 cup of motor oil to saturate the sand. Plunge dirty garden tools into the sand. The sand scours away the mud and the oil helps prevent the tools from rusting.

HOME CARE & REPAIR

➤ Use sand to **create a rough surface.** When painting exterior or basement steps, mix a little bit of sand with your paint and you'll have a gritty surface with less chance of slipping.

HOUSEKEEPING

➤ Sand can **substitute for an extra set of hands** when fixing a broken handle on a teacup or coffee mug or a cracked or broken dish. Fill a small tub with about 6 inches of sand, and put the broken dish in it with the area that needs repair sticking up out of the sand. The sand will hold the piece firmly so you have both hands free to work.

IN THE KITCHEN

➤ **Eliminate rust in your cast-iron pots and pans** by sprinkling some sand over the rust, mix in some vegetable oil, and rub with a little elbow grease. This should clean away the rust in no time. Wash well before using.

Shampoo & Shower Caps

Both shampoo and shower caps can be used all over the house, not just in the bathroom.

PERSONAL CARE

➤ Use shampoo to **clean your hairbrush.** Fill your sink with hot water, add two tablespoons of shampoo, and let your brushes and combs soak for an hour or so. Then just rinse them clean.

STAIN REMOVAL

➤ **Get rid of those greasy-looking spots left behind by liquid fabric softener:** Dab the spots with a little shampoo and wash in cold water.

HOME CARE & REPAIR

➤ Use a little squirt of shampoo as a **substitute for dishwashing liquid** in the sink.

➤ **Create a mini greenhouse indoors.** When you're going away for a few days, water your plants and then cover them with a shower cap. This will keep the plants moist.

➤ Attach a shower cap to the bottom of a hanging plant. It will **catch drips when you water plants.**

IN THE KITCHEN

➤ If you run out of plastic wrap, **cover leftover food** by placing a new, unused shower cap over the dish.

➤ Use a shower cap to **cover food in the microwave**—no more splatters.

Shaving Cream

The conditioning and cleaning properties of white shaving cream make it useful all around the house. Buy a few cans to keep in your workroom, shed, and garage.

HOME CARE & REPAIR

➤ To **repair a squeaky door,** use a nail set and a hammer to loosen the hinge pin. Rub some shaving cream over the pin and reinstall it. That should silence the squeak.

HOUSEKEEPING

➤ White shaving cream is also a great **spot remover for carpets and upholstery,** especially for coffee, tea, and makeup stains. Spray a small amount on the spot and dab with a damp white cloth until you see the stain lifting.

➤ Shaving cream **cleans dirt and grime off of your hands** without water. Spray some on, and rub your hands together, then wipe off the shaving cream. It also will **remove dried latex paint from your skin.**

➤ **Condition a new baseball glove** for a fraction of the cost of a glove conditioner by rubbing shaving cream into the surface.

Mrs. Fixit's
AMAZING!
If you use up all of the shaving cream testing these tips, use a smidgen of hair conditioner for shaving until you get to the store.
Personal Care Tip

A B C D E F G H I J K L M N O P Q R S T U V W X Y Z

Shoe Polish

If pulling out all of your staining supplies for a small wood project seems like it will be a bigger mess than it's worth, grab your shoe shine kit instead.

HOME CARE & REPAIR

➤ For small projects, plain shoe polish is a great **substitute for traditional wood stains.** Brown polish will give you a walnut look, cordovan will mimic cherry or mahogany, and you'll get a light maple finish with tan polish. Make sure the piece has been sanded smooth and all of the dust has been wiped away.
Use a soft cloth to wipe the polish over the piece. You'll get the best coverage if you use nice long strokes and make sure you blend in any polish clumps so you have a smooth finish. Allow the polish to seep into the wood and dry overnight. Once it's dry, you can carefully add a second coat of polish. Again, make sure you smooth it out for a nice finish.

TIP: Once both coats have dried completely, coat with paste wax for a great shine.

Socks

Make those mismatched socks march to a different drummer!

HOUSEKEEPING

➤ **Prevent scuffs and scratches on your floor** when you move heavy furniture. Slip a cotton sock over the leg of each piece that you're moving and you'll be surprised at how easily it slides along the floor.

➤ Instead of a cloth, slip a sock over your hand to **dust furniture.** Spray the sock and start polishing. It covers large areas quickly, and you can use your fingers to get into little nooks and crevices. If you're in a hurry, just slip a sock over each hand and you'll be able to work twice as fast.

➤ **Prevent fingerprints on freshly polished silver** by slipping socks over your hands. Socks are nice and soft for polishing, plus your hands are covered so you won't leave fingerprints.

HOME CARE & REPAIR

➤ **Use a sock for a paint mitt.** Put a rubber glove on your hand and slip the sock over that. You'll be able to paint curvy surfaces easily and efficiently; when you're done, just pull the sock inside out and throw it away.

> *Mrs. Fixit's*
>
> To prevent mismatched socks in the first place, use a diaper pin (which won't rust) to hold pairs of socks together in the laundry.
>
> *Laundry Tip*

Steel Wool

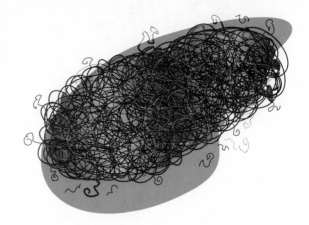

Scrub more than just pots and pans with steel wool.

IN THE WORKSHOP

➤ If you have a screw hole that has become too big for the screw, stuff it with steel wool. An awl or a long nail can help get the steel wool into the hole. Reinsert the screw. The steel wool will **grip the screw just like wood.**

➤ Steel wool is indispensable in the workshop. It comes in seven grades ranging from coarse to superfine, and it can be used for everything from **removing paint to polishing metal to woodworking.**

HOME CARE & REPAIR

➤ If pests are a problem in your house, stuff steel wool in and around the pipes under sinks; this will **keep pests to a minimum.**

➤ **Prefill holes on the exterior of your home before you caulk**—steel wool is an economical filler.

HOUSEKEEPING

➤ Stuff some steel wool in the toe of an old sock and tie the sock off to **create an instant pincushion** that will keep pins and needles rust free and nice and sharp!

➤ Put steel wool in your tub drain to **catch fur and prevent clogs when you give your pet a bath.**

Mrs. Fixit's

AMAZING!

To prevent a rusty mess by your sink, store a partially used steely wool pad in a plastic bag or aluminum foil in the freezer; it will last longer.

Housekeeping Tip

Tape

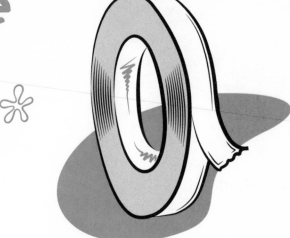

From masking tape to packing tape, keep plenty around the house to make chores easier.

IN THE WORKSHOP

➤ **Reduce splintering your wood when you saw** by running a length of masking tape along your cut line.

➤ If you're having trouble holding a screw when starting it, stick the end through a piece of masking tape and tape it to the screwdriver. You can **drive a screw without dropping it** and pull the tape off when you're done!

➤ Before you start a project with a sanding block, put a strip of wide packaging or duct tape on the back of your sandpaper. This will give you a cutting guide because it is just the right width and will **keep your paper from ripping on the block as you sand.**

HOUSEKEEPING

➤ **Make a trap for silverfish** by running double-sided tape up the side of a glass and putting it upright where you spot the bugs. They'll climb up the tape and once they're in the glass they won't be able to climb out.

➤ Before you **hang a picture on plaster walls,** crisscross some transparent tape over the spot where you are going to drive the nail. It will prevent the nail from cracking the wall.

Tea & Tea Bags

After you've brewed
up a cup, collect the leaves
for use around your household.

IN THE YARD
➤ **Fertilize the soil** with tea leaves. You can work used
tea leaves into the soil for a nourishing treat,
or dilute a cup of tea in four cups of water
and use it to water your plants.

HOUSEKEEPING
➤ Cold tea is a great **cleaner for wood;** just brew
up a big batch in the morning and let it cool. Use the
tea and a soft cloth to clean your cabinets. It will cut
right through the grime.

➤ To **clean your mirrors,** try a little cold tea. Just dip
a lint-free cloth into the tea and scrub the surface.
Wipe dry for a sparkling reflection.

IN THE GARAGE
➤ To **keep dust to a minimum when sweeping,** wet
three or four tea bags and rip them open. Sprinkle the
damp tea leaves on the floor before you start sweeping;
it will make the job a lot easier.

Tennis Balls

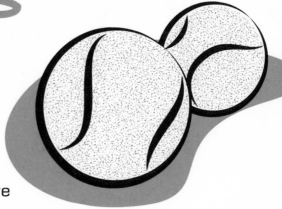

Tennis balls can be used for more than just a game; I have some great alternative uses that will come in handy all over your house.

HOME CARE
➤ To easily **remove a lightbulb that has broken off in a socket,** turn off the power at the electrical panel or unplug the lamp. Push a tennis ball against the broken socket and twist the remains out with ease.

➤ Tennis balls are an asset in the laundry room. Not only can they be tossed into the dryer to **give new life to a comforter, some curtains, or a jacket,** but a new tennis ball will also **help fight static in the laundry.** Just toss it in the dryer with the rest of the clothes.

IN THE WORKSHOP
➤ **Protect surfaces** when you hammer. Cut a slit in a tennis ball and **slip it over the hammer head for an instant mallet.** Or **slip it onto the legs of a chair to prevent it from scratching the floor.**

IN THE GARAGE
➤ **The ball marks the spot in the garage** if you're not sure how far you should pull in. Put the car where it is supposed to be and suspend a tennis ball from the ceiling so it rests on the windshield. This way you can pull into the garage and know just when to stop.

Tiles

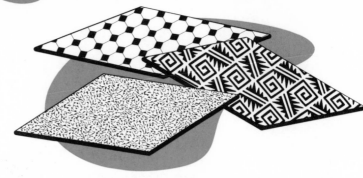

Every tiling project has leftovers; here's a few good ideas for putting those loose tiles to work.

HOUSEKEEPING

➤ Use some tiles to **trim a stock window box,** and use the box as attractive and coordinating storage in a room.

➤ Glue a layer of cork or felt to the bottom of a ceramic tile and **create a hot plate or coaster** to protect your furniture.

➤ Use broken tiles to help **drainage in the bottom of plant pots.**

IN THE KITCHEN

➤ Keep a few ceramic tiles in the kitchen. When you're getting ready to serve dinner, heat them in the oven for a few minutes. Use them **as warmers in the bottom of bread and roll baskets**. (Make sure you use potholders to handle the warm tiles.)

> **TIP:** Don't get too carried away and use all of your leftover tiles. You should always keep a few tiles on hand just in case you end up with a chipped or broken tile that needs repair.

Toothpaste

The cleaning and brightening power of white toothpaste doesn't work on teeth only—it has some surprising alternative uses too!

HOUSEKEEPING

➤ Quickly **shine chrome faucets in the bathroom** using a dab of white toothpaste on a soft cloth. It's a quick and easy way to clean up the faucets using what's right at your fingertips.

➤ **Buff out white rings on wood furniture** caused by moisture trapped in the surface of the wood. The mild abrasive found in white toothpaste buffs them out in no time. Gently work the paste into the ring with a dry cloth, then wipe it up with a slightly damp cloth; the ring will disappear.

➤ **To clean glass-top stoves,** just use a dab of white toothpaste, a little water, and scrub with a cloth. Your stovetop will be clean in no time.

HOME CARE & REPAIR

➤ Use toothpaste to **fill a nail hole in your wall** when you're out of surfacing compound. Toothpaste hardens just like regular nail fillers; when it dries, touch up the spot with a touch of paint.

KID STUFF

➤ Small children love to color—and it seems places like walls and woodwork are irresistible to them! A damp cloth and a little white toothpaste will **erase crayon drawings** in no time flat.

A B C D E F G H I J K L M N O P Q R S T U V W X Y Z

Toothpicks

If you're looking for an easy way to solve some common household dilemmas, grab a toothpick.

HOME CARE & REPAIR
➤ Use a toothpick to **mark the end of a roll of tape.** Pull out the amount of tape you need and stick a toothpick to the underside of the end of the tape. It will hold the tape so you can cut it, and leave it under the tip so you'll have a handy pull tab the next time you need the tape.

➤ **If you don't want to lose your nail holes** when repainting, pop a section of toothpick in each hole after you remove the nail while you're prepping a room. You'll know exactly where to rehang the pictures after the room is painted.

IN THE WORKSHOP
➤ To **fill a hole in wood,** stick a toothpick in the hole, break it off, and sand it smooth. Then use wood putty. You'll use less putty, there will be less shrinkage, and you'll end up with a smoother patch in the long run.

➤ Use a toothpick to **apply glue in small or intricate areas.**

IN THE KITCHEN
➤ Keep some toothpicks by the sink; they're great to **clean little crevices in garlic presses, graters, and kids' sippy cups.**

Turkey Baster

This is another one of those kitchen gadgets that seems to come out only once a year. But you'll want a couple of extra basters to use around the house.

IN THE YARD
➤ When packing up your lawn mower for the winter season you need to empty it because old gas will harm your engine. Use an old turkey baster to **suction the gas out of your lawn mower.** (Put it in a gas can and bring it to a car repair shop, or call your local health department for disposal guidelines.)

HOUSEKEEPING
➤ Suck some water up into a turkey baster and use it to **water out-of-reach plants.** You won't have to climb to water plants ever again.

➤ When you're ready to take down your Christmas tree, use a turkey baster to **remove leftover water from the Christmas tree stand** so it doesn't spill all over the floor.

IN THE KITCHEN
➤ **Make perfect pancakes** with this clever idea: Suction batter into the baster and squeeze it out onto a hot griddle.

➤ Quickly **clean up a dropped egg.** Suck it up with a turkey baster and squirt it down the disposal for an easy cleanup.

Twist Ties

Save the twist ties from bread, and the extras from rolls of plastic garbage bags—you'll be surprised how many uses these little items have.

HOUSEKEEPING

➤ Use twist ties to **manage the wires under your desk or behind your media equipment!**

➤ If the screw that holds together your eyeglasses falls out, use the wire from a twist tie to **hold your glasses together** until you can get to the optical shop for a repair. Simply peel the paper off a twist tie; the little wire inside is the perfect size for a quick fix.

➤ **Keep your suitcase zipper secure** on a trip by threading a twist tie through the holes. It's the perfect makeshift luggage latch.

➤ A twist tie **makes a handy zipper pull** when the zip tab disappears.

➤ In a pinch, use a twist tie as a **hanger on the back of a wreath.**

IN THE GARDEN

➤ Use a twist tie to **secure a climbing plant to a garden structure or trellis** while training the vines.

➤ Twist ties are also good for **securing small plants to their stakes** when a little extra support is needed.

Mrs. Fixit's

AMAZING!

If you're looking for the freshest bread at the grocery store check the twist ties:
Monday – BLUE
Tuesday – GREEN
Thursday – RED
Friday – WHITE
Saturday – YELLOW

Housekeeping Tip

Vanilla

A staple for baking, vanilla can do more than flavor cookies.

HOME CARE & REPAIR
➤ Add 2 teaspoons of vanilla extract to 1 gallon of paint and stir well. The vanilla will help **neutralize paint fumes.**

HOUSEKEEPING
➤ Soak some cotton balls with vanilla to **make a homemade air freshener.** Just pop them into your vacuum bag. Every time you run the machine, that great smell will waft around the room.

IN THE KITCHEN
➤ To **keep the fridge smelling good,** soak a paper towel with vanilla extract and wipe down the walls of the fridge.

➤ To **give coffee a nice flavor,** add a couple of drops of vanilla extract to the grounds before you brew.

A B C D E F G H I J K L M N O P Q R S T U V W X Y Z

Vegetable Peeler

Sure your vegetable peeler is handy when you're making a salad, but think outside the bowl for some easy solutions to frustrating household problems.

IN THE WORKSHOP
➤ The pointy tip of a vegetable peeler is an ideal tool for **tightening a loose screw** when you don't have a phillips screwdriver on hand.

HOUSEKEEPING
➤ No pencil sharpener? No problem! **Use a vegetable peeler to bring that pencil back to a point.** This works especially well on carpenter's pencils!

➤ Candles too big for the holders? Don't worry: a peeler will help you **take off just enough wax for the candle to fit snugly.**

IN THE GARDEN
➤ Put a vegetable peeler with your garden tools its pointy end can dig in to **loosen the roots of stubborn weeds,** or you could measure the blade end and **use it as a handy depth guide when planting seeds.**

IN THE KITCHEN
➤ You can use a vegetable peeler to **shave small slivers from cheese, butter, chocolate or citrus fruits** for various recipes.

Mrs. Fixit's
AMAZING!

Use an old toothbrush to scrub the convex blade of your vegetable peeler to keep it nice and clean!

Kitchen Tip

Vegetable Shortening

In these fat-free days, the container of vegetable shortening hiding in the back of the fridge usually comes out only for making holiday pies. Here are some ideas for using it year-round.

STAIN REMOVAL

➤ Vegetable shortening magically **removes ink from all sorts of household surfaces.** Use a soft cloth to spread a little over ink smears on vinyl, plastic, appliances, and skin. Let it sit for a minute or so, then wipe the ink away.

➤ **Remove lipstick stains on linens and clothes** with vegetable shortening. Spread a thick layer onto the lipstick stain and allow it to sit for five minutes. Rub some detergent into the shortening and launder the garment as usual.

IN THE YARD

➤ **Remove the sticky mess that sap and tar leave on garden tools** using superfine steel wool and a generous dollop of vegetable shortening. Work the steel wool in small circles until the sap is removed. As a bonus, the shortening lubricates your garden tools.

PERSONAL CARE

➤ **Get sticky stuff off your skin** by rubbing shortening into your skin. Wash thoroughly with soap and water afterward.

➤ If you have sensitive skin, try vegetable shortening **as a natural moisturizer.** Simply slather it on to heal dry, itchy skin.

A B C D E F G H I J K L M N O P Q R S T U V W X Y Z

Vinegar

Forget the little bottle of white vinegar—you'll want to buy this household wonder by the gallon.

HOUSEKEEPING

➤ To help **preserve fresh-cut flowers** add 2 tablespoons of white vinegar and 2 tablespoons of sugar to the vase with your water. The vinegar will kill bacteria and the sugar will feed the flowers.

➤ Warm white vinegar in the microwave for 30 seconds and use it to **break through hardened soap scum and hard water stains** in your bath and shower.

➤ **Clean out jets and hoses in your dishwasher and washing machine.** Put a cup of white vinegar in an empty machine and run it through a cycle.

➤ Add white vinegar to a full load of laundry and it will **soften, deodorize, and delint clothes.** It will also **help remove excess soap,** which can cause skin irritation.

HOME CARE & REPAIR

➤ **Fix flow problems on the faucets** by simply soaking a towel in white vinegar and wrapping it around the fixture. Leave it for an hour and scrub the deposits away with an old toothbrush.

➤ Mix 3 tablespoons of vinegar into 1 quart of water and use it to **clean cloudy buildup from wood furniture and floors.**

IN THE GARAGE

➤ A cloth dipped in white vinegar will easily **clean road grime from your windshield wipers.**

Mrs. Fixit's
AMAZING!

Slow drain? Pour 1 cup of baking soda down the drain followed by 1 cup of white vinegar. When the two have stopped fizzing, dump 1 gallon of boiling water down the drain to flush it clean. Use this solution once a month to prevent clogs from forming. It also works for septic systems.

Home Tip

Vodka

Raise a glass to these clever ideas for using vodka around the house.

HOUSEKEEPING

➤ Use vodka to **clean gold and gemstone jewelry.** Soak your jewels in a shot glass of vodka, then scrub clean with a soft toothbrush. The vodka will dissolve grime and leave your rocks with a little more bling.

➤ If you're having people over and you've run out of bathroom cleaner pour, some vodka into a spray bottle. It will quickly **shine chrome fixtures and mirrors** and will **remove stains from bathtub caulk.**

➤ Vodka can also benefit your fresh-cut flowers. Pour a tablespoon or so into the water in your vase, it will **kill bacteria that can harm your flowers** and keep the water nice and clean.

➤ Anytime you cut bulb flowers such as tulips or daffodils, mix together 3 cups of water and 1 tablespoon of vodka. The vodka will **keep the stems of the flowers nice and firm** so that you don't end up with slumped-over blooms. Gives new meaning to a stiff drink.

A B C D E F G H I J K L M N O P Q R S T U V W X Y Z

Wallpaper Books

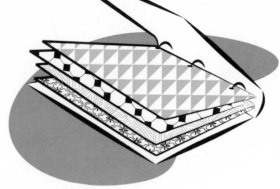

Check your local wallpaper store for out-of-date wallpaper books and bring a couple home for these creative uses.

> **TIP:** *To use a page from one of these books, remove it with a straightedge and a utility knife. You may also want to cut off any damaged edges from people looking through the books.*

HOUSEKEEPING

➤ Wallpaper's beautiful prints **lend themselves easily to creating gift wrap.** Cut out a page and use it to wrap your gift. If you aren't comfortable using the actual page, make a color photocopy.

➤ **Line your kitchen and bedroom drawers** by simply cutting the pages to size.

➤ Use your straightedge and utility knife to cut wallpaper page down to **create a mat for your favorite pictures.**

➤ Cut sections from the wallpaper and frame them to **make inexpensive artwork** in your home.

IN THE KITCHEN

➤ Laminate a few coordinating sheets to **create kitchen place mats.** If you have leftover paper from wallpapering the kitchen, you can make a complete matching set for the table!

Mrs. Fixit's AMAZING!

For a grease stain on your wallpaper, grab the baby powder, rub it into the spot, and let it sit for a while. Then, brush away the spot with a soft paintbrush.

Housekeeping Tip

Waxed Paper

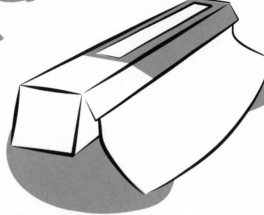

A longtime kitchen favorite, waxed paper has many uses throughout the house.

HOME CARE & REPAIR

➤ To **prevent a skin from forming on your paint** while it's in storage, put the can on a sheet of waxed paper and trace the size. Cut out the circle and place it directly on the surface of the paint in the can. This will protect the paint and keep it fresh.

➤ **Keep your car antenna moving smoothly** by rubbing it with waxed paper.

IN THE WORKSHOP

➤ **Keep saw blades sliding smoothly** by rubbing waxed paper along the edges.

IN THE KITCHEN

➤ **Clean a can opener.** Crunch a piece of waxed paper in the wheel mechanism on your can opener and crank the handle to clean and sharpen in one quick twist.

HOUSEKEEPING

➤ Use waxed paper to **create a pattern for small sewing projects.** Just trace your shapes onto the paper and cut them out.

Whitewall Tire Cleaner
(Tire Whitener)

The same ingredient that whitens your tire's whitewalls can whiten and brighten all kinds of things and clean up messy problems.

HOUSEKEEPING

➤ **Clean your fireplace.** Use some whitewall cleaner to scrub soot and deposits off the brick; rinse well.

➤ Try **cleaning grout** that looks beyond saving with some whitewall cleaner and an old toothbrush.

STAIN REMOVAL

➤ Use whitewall cleaner to **remove stains from vinyl on boats, campers, and trailers.**

➤ **Remove stains on white vinyl tile.** Spray it on and scrub clean.

IN THE KITCHEN

➤ **Clean the burnt-on food from your stovetop.** Spray the cleaner over the mess and wipe it away with a scrubber sponge.

> TIP: *When using tire whitener, make sure you read and follow the safety instructions on the packaging.*

Yogurt & Yogurt Containers

Yogurt and those perfect plastic cups are useful everywhere in the house.

IN THE YARD

➤ If you like that timeworn weathered look, **paint rocks, terra-cotta pots, and bricks** with plain yogurt to encourage moss.

➤ Use clean yogurt containers to **start seedlings.**

HOUSEKEEPING

➤ Use a dollop of yogurt to **clean dingy ivory piano keys.** Simply wipe on a small amount, and buff it off.

KID STUFF

➤ **Make safe fingerpaints for kids** by tinting plain yogurt with food coloring. (Don't do this if your child is allergic to dairy products.)

> **TIP:** *Because yogurt is a dairy product, it will spoil. Pop "fingerpaints" in the fridge if kids walk away for a few minutes. Throw away remaining yogurt paint when they're finished.*

➤ A yogurt container is the perfect size to **send a snack to school in a lunchbox.** Fill it with crackers, cereal, or a sweet treat!

➤ Use the containers to **organize art supplies.**

IN THE KITCHEN

➤ Fill an empty yogurt container with baking soda, poke holes in the cover and stash it in the refrigerator, closet, or basement to **keep odors at bay.**

REPURPOSING PROJECTS

* * * * * * * * *

Wait! Don't throw it out!

You can reuse, revamp or

repurpose it. Use it for something

else! There are uses for

discarded items that can save

you money. "It's just that simple!"

* * * * * * * * *

A B C D E F G H I J K L M N O P Q R S T U V W X Y Z

ARCHITECTURAL MIRRORS

It's all the rage to mimic architectural pieces for accessorizing homes. Here's an easy way to make a mirror out of a ceiling medallion.

1. Pick up a reproduction ceiling medallion at your local home improvement center. They cost between $5 and $10.

2. Prime and paint the medallion with two coats of acrylic paint. (If your medallion is made of plastic or resin, be sure to use a bonding primer.)

3. Now for the mirror. Trace the opening of the medallion to use as a template to be sure that you're getting the right size. (TIP: If you hit your local discount store you can pick up a mirror for under a dollar—much less than at a home center or a glass store, and they come in a bunch of different sizes.)

4. Remove any framing pieces from the mirror, and simply secure it to the back side of the medallion using mirror adhesive.

ART ON A BUDGET

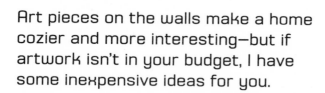

Art pieces on the walls make a home cozier and more interesting—but if artwork isn't in your budget, I have some inexpensive ideas for you.

➤ Buy a calendar with pictures that you like. For about $10, you have 12 potential prints to frame for your walls. Pick up some mat board and standard-size frames, and you have artwork for very little money.

➤ For smaller pieces, check out your local card store. There are so many great cards today, and many of them fit easily into standard-size frames.

➤ Another place to check for low-cost artwork: the china cabinet. Plate hangers cost about a dollar apiece and hanging your seldom-used china on the walls makes a beautiful addition to your home decor.

> **TIP:** *If you don't want to use your china check your local discount store for closeout platters and plates.*

➤ A perennial favorite, wreaths also make a nice statement and can be made inexpensively with items from your local craft store.

➤ For kids' rooms, use themed items: For a boy's room, sports equipment; for a girl's room, try some outgrown dresses on a clothesline.

A
B
C
D
E
F
G
H
I
J
K
L
M
N
O
P
Q
R
S
T
U
V
W
X
Y
Z

BOTTLE LAMP

If you come across an interesting old bottle or jug but don't know what to do with it, why not turn it into a lamp? It's easy to do. Simply buy a lamp kit designed to use with a bottle, which you'll find at any home improvement center.

➤ Wash your bottle and allow it to dry completely.

1. Figure out which cork adapter fits into your bottle. (The kit will come with small, medium and large adaptors.) Thread the small metal rod in the kit through the bottom of the adapter until it extends ¼ inch, then twist the small locknut into place.

2. Insert the adapter into the bottle opening; slide the base ring and socket cap over the rod.

3. Thread the lamp cord through the socket cap and pull it out leaving at least a few inches of wire. Split the cord wires in two and create an underwriter's knot (see *Repurposing Tip*).

4. Connect the wires to the terminal screws on the socket. Wrap the wire with smooth insulation clockwise around the brass screw; then wrap the wire with the ribbed insulation clockwise around the silver screw. Tighten screws.

5. Push the socket shell and cardboard insulation over the wiring until you hear a faint click so you know it's secure. Put a bulb in, plug the cord in, and test your lamp.

TIP: *Follow the directions that come with your kit if you have any questions.*

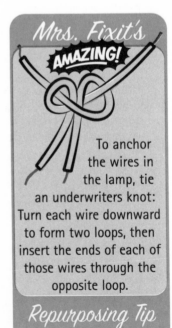

Mrs. Fixit's AMAZING!

To anchor the wires in the lamp, tie an underwriters knot: Turn each wire downward to form two loops, then insert the ends of each of those wires through the opposite loop.

Repurposing Tip

BUREAU TO KITCHEN ISLAND

If you have a chest of drawers you're no longer using, turn it into a baking center. It's an easy project that costs just a fraction of buying a kitchen island, and it's a one-of-a kind piece.

> If the dresser is in good shape, simply leave it as is and use the drawers for storage.

> To make the dresser meld better with the room, follow these steps:

1. Remove the bottom two drawers, cut a piece of MDF board to fit into the drawer glides and use L brackets to secure the boards to the frame.

2. Attach some stock molding to the front of the shelves with finishing nails.

3. Paint the entire piece so that it fits into your kitchen's color scheme.

4. To make the piece more versatile, tile the top or cover it with stainless steel so you can use it as a resting place for hot pots and dishes.

> TIP: *You'll want to choose an old dresser that's about the same height as your kitchen counters—between 32 and 36 inches.*

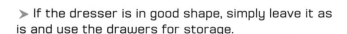

CHINA MOSAIC

Old pieces of mismatched or broken china are a great starting point to create a mirror, a picture frame, tabletop, or even a tray. Make sure you have heavy gloves and safety glasses before you start.

1. Wrap old pieces of china in a towel or canvas tarp and use a hammer to break them down into smaller pieces. You can use whatever size you want, but pieces smaller than 2 inches is difficult to work with.

2. For a tray or table, you'll need to build up a lip around the edge with some molding, then clean any dust and dirt off the area. You're ready to start.

3. Figure out a pattern and use tile adhesive to stick the pieces in place. If working on a large flat area use a notched trowel to apply the adhesive. Make sure the pieces are about $\frac{1}{4}$ inch apart so you have room for grout.

4. Mix the grout according to the directions on the package and apply it with a grout float, working it into all of the crevices.

5. Wait about 15 minutes and then use a damp sponge to remove excess grout for a clean surface.

6. When it is completely set, use a towel to polish the pieces of china to get rid of hazy film.

CHRISTMAS STORAGE

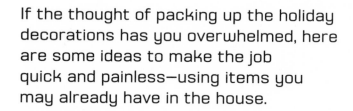

If the thought of packing up the holiday decorations has you overwhelmed, here are some ideas to make the job quick and painless—using items you may already have in the house.

➤ Make sure that you remove hangers from the ornaments each year. If moisture gets into the boxes the hangers could rust and ruin those treasures.

➤ To pack up regular glass bulb ornaments, use sock dividers. You can buy them at most housewares stores. Sock dividers separate and protect the ornaments so they don't get broken. Or check with your local liquor store. Liquor is shipped in sectioned boxes to protect the bottles, so you might just get some great storage for free.

➤ Another good way to protect ornaments is to pack boxes in boxes. Small plastic shoeboxes will hold fragile ornaments safely. Then pack all of the smaller boxes into one big box.

➤ Wind lights around plastic ribbon spools. This keeps them untangled and easy to pull off next year.

➤ If you save packing peanuts from holiday shipping, you have great buffers for fragile decorations.

➤ Cover large trees or decorations with plastic garbage bags to protect them from dust and dirt throughout the year.

A B C D E F G H I J K L M N O P Q R S T U V W X Y Z

CLOCK MAKING

A clock is a basic necessity in any home, but finding one that matches your decor can be a challenge. That's not a problem: I can tell you how to make a custom clock in no time flat.

➤ Choose an item to use for your clock: a decorative plate, a tile, wood, or a toy—the possibilities are endless, so be creative.

1. Measure the thickness of the item. Take the measurement with you to any craft or hardware store, and purchase a clockworks kit with the appropriate-size shaft.

2. If you're making your clock from a decorative plate or tile, use a glass or tile bit on your drill to put a hole in the center of the piece. Always remember safety glasses when using your drill.

3. Once you've drilled the hole, clean away any dust and debris and put the shaft of the mechanism through the piece from back to front.

4. When the mechanism is securely in place, assemble the clock face on the front, add a battery, and you're done.

5. At this point you can add embellishments if you'd like to make the clock your own.

CLUTTER BUSTERS

If clutter just seems to appear around your home and you can't get a handle on it, here are some handy clutter busters to help you out.

➤ When the mail comes, sort it right away. Toss the junk mail. File mail that you need to tend to in a napkin holder; it will still be visible so you don't forget about it, but it looks nice and neat.

➤ Piles of place mats? Clip them together with a large binder clip and hang them on a cup hook inside a cabinet or pantry.

➤ Use cup hooks to keep keys off the counter. Simply screw a couple of hooks on the inside of the closet door. This way you can hang up your keys when you hang up jackets and handbags. Keys are out of the way, and you'll always know where they are.

➤ Save yourself those 10 trips up and down the stairs every day: Get a stair basket. Simply stash things inside that need to go upstairs in the basket, and bring it with you once a day!

➤ If you're plain short on storage space, take advantage of the space under furniture. For example, store items in plastic shoeboxes and then stash them under a bed or a skirted couch or chair. This is also a perfect spot for extra leaves from your dining table; just be sure you have carpet (or slip a pad under the leaves) so you don't scratch the surface when you slide the leaves in and out.

A B C D E F G H I J K L M N O P Q R S T U V W X Y Z

CONTAINER GARDENING

If you'd like to have a garden but don't have much space, consider container gardening.

➤ The key to a successful container garden is the potting soil. There are many brands on the market, but you can also mix your own. Combine two parts of peat moss with one part of builder's sand.

➤ Think outside the box, or pot, when you're choosing your container—just be sure to provide good drainage. Be creative: Anything from baskets to old shoes, to pottery can find new life as a container for your garden.

➤ Choose your plants carefully. Put plants with similar temperaments in the same pot: Group sun and water lovers together in one pot and shade lovers in another.

➤ Don't forget to put drainage material in the bottom of your container. Broken terra-cotta pots, packing peanuts, and pebbles are good choices.

➤ Add potting soil, arrange your plants, and fill with additional soil around the perimeter.

➤ Once your container is finished, water it well. I like to dissolve an envelope of unflavored gelatin in a quart of water and feed my plants with this mixture. It makes a nitrogen-rich plant food that also helps the plant retain water.

TIP: Container gardens are great accents for any outdoor space!

DEODORIZERS

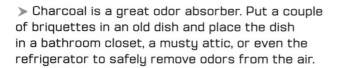
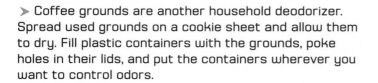

You don't need to buy fancy deodorizers to keep your rooms smelling fresh. You probably have some natural alternatives around the house.

➤ Charcoal is a great odor absorber. Put a couple of briquettes in an old dish and place the dish in a bathroom closet, a musty attic, or even the refrigerator to safely remove odors from the air.

➤ Coffee grounds are another household deodorizer. Spread used grounds on a cookie sheet and allow them to dry. Fill plastic containers with the grounds, poke holes in their lids, and put the containers wherever you want to control odors.

➤ Kitty litter has natural deodorizing properties. Put a container or two in the basement, laundry room—even in old suitcases—to keep them smelling clean and fresh.

➤ Vanilla is also a great deodorizer and adds a fresh scent to spaces. Soak cotton balls with vanilla extract and store them in closets and pantries.

➤ Believe it or not, onions will also work as a deodorizer in special circumstances. Cut a couple of onions in half and put them on plates around a freshly painted room. The onions absorb the paint fumes and odors, making the room easier on the nose right after painting.

A B C D E F G H I J K L M N O P Q R S T U V W X Y Z

DINING TO CRAFTING
REPURPOSE
A TABLE

Rather than getting rid of an old dining room table and chairs, simply move them to your craft or project room.

➤ If your table accommodates leaves, it's perfect for projects! Try these tips.

1. Whenever you need to cut a straight line in fabrics, poster board, wrapping paper—whatever!—simply pull the table apart about 1/4 inch for a perfectly straight cutting line.

2. Make measuring easy by gluing a stainless-steel yardstick to the top of the table, just to the left of the center cutting line.

3. Most housewares stores carry "drawers" made of a white metal mesh that you can screw to the underside of cabinet shelves. Pick up a couple of those and screw them into the underside of the table to organize supplies.

4. Put the old table leaves to work too. Use large shelf brackets to mount the now unnecessary leaves to the wall for extra shelving.

DOUBLE~DUTY KITCHEN GADGETS

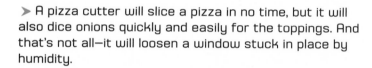

You probably have a drawer full of one-use gadgets—but don't limit them simply to the task they were designed for when there are so many alternative uses.

➤ A pizza cutter will slice a pizza in no time, but it will also dice onions quickly and easily for the toppings. And that's not all—it will loosen a window stuck in place by humidity.

➤ An ice cream scoop is the perfect size for measuring pancake batter and portioning no-mess muffins or put an old scoop to use in the garden. Use it to scoop soil into small pots for plantings.

➤ Speaking of muffins, use that muffin tin to hold baked potatoes or stuffed peppers upright in the oven.

➤ Muffin pans are also an easy sick tray for kids in bed.

➤ An egg slicer does a great job of slicing mushrooms and strawberries.

➤ Use a strawberry huller to separate coffee filters and baking cups with ease—no more frustration with them sticking together.

➤ An old ice-cube tray can be used almost anywhere in the house to organize pills, jewelry, nails, or screws.

➤ Use an old fork to hold up a recipe card or to pull weeds in your garden.

ABCDEFGHIJKLMNOPQRSTUVWXYZ

ETCHING GLASS

Etching is an easy and inexpensive way to add new life to glass. Try it on windows, mirrors, or glass-front cabinets.

> **TIP:** *First, safety! Etching cream is toxic. Wear safety glasses, a respirator mask, long sleeves, and rubber gloves when working with the cream.*

1. Work in a well-ventilated area. Clean and dry the glass so it is completely clear of dust, dirt, and grease.

2. For a custom design, cut stencils from contact paper and apply the stencils directly to the glass. Be sure to press the edges of the stencil firmly to get a nice crisp result. Of course, you can also simply etch the whole panel of glass to create a frosted look.

3. Apply the etching cream onto your glass in a thick even coat using a paintbrush.

4. Let it sit for five minutes or so to react with the glass. (Check specific directions on the etching product packaging.)

5. Wash the cream away completely with water and a clean sponge.

EVERYDAY FRUSTRATIONS

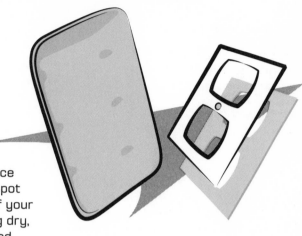

A little clever thinking can eliminate some of life's little aggravations. Here are just a few quick-and-easy solutions to make your life easier.

➤ Put your marbles to good use! Place a few marbles in the bottom of a teapot to prevent lime buildup. As a bonus, if your teapot is dangerously close to boiling dry, you'll hear the marbles banging around.

➤ Stop snagging sheer curtains as you pull them over the rod by slipping the finger of a rubber glove over the end of the curtain rod. The fabric will slide over the glove instead of getting caught on the metal.

➤ Block the draft from leaky outlets. Thoroughly clean the plastic foam from a package of meat from the grocery store. Then use the outlet cover as a template to cut an insulating pad from the plastic foam. Reinstall the outlet cover—with its new foam insulation—to stop the draft.

➤ Do your candles tip back and forth in your candleholder? Cut apart a wide rubber band, wrap it around the base of your candle, and put the candle back into its holder. It will stand up nice and straight. If you don't have a rubber band, try pushing the flat head of a pushpin into the side of a candle base to use as a spacer.

➤ Are you using too much laundry detergent to pretreat stains on clothing? Take an empty dishwashing liquid squeeze bottle and fill it with laundry detergent. The bottle will allow you to squeeze as little or as much detergent as necessary to fight your stain.

FLOOR~ CLOTH

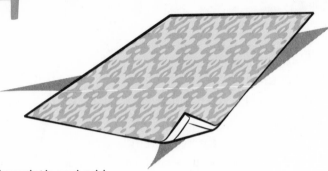

Get a custom floor treatment without spending a lot of money—floorcloths are quick and easy!

1. Determine the final size of your floorcloth and add 1 inch to the width and 1 inch to the length. Cut the canvas and turn the edges under ½ inch on each side. Hem the canvas to the final size using iron-on hem tape. (You'll find canvas at fabric and craft stores. Or use a painter's drop cloth—if you use the whole piece, it's already hemmed!)

2. Prime one side of the canvas and let it dry. Prime the other side. When the primer is dry, paint a base color on the top side of the cloth using a regular roller and latex paint. You may need two coats to get the color right.

3. Now all you have to do is paint the pattern or accent color of your choice. Use latex or acrylic paint and your imagination. Stencils and stamps are a great way to get a perfect design every time. If you're feeling artistic, try painting freehand.

4. To make a border, measure in from the edge the desired depth all around the perimeter of the cloth; using a carpenter's square will help you with this step. Tape off the measurement using painter's tape. Use a small roller or brush to paint the border. Let the paint dry completely and peel off the tape.

5. Spray the painted floorcloth with a couple of coats of polyurethane to protect it.

TIP: *Floorcloths don't always grip the floor, so always use a safety pad under your floorcloth.*

FOOLPROOF BED SKIRT

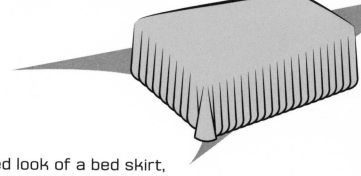

If you like the finished look of a bed skirt, here's an easy alternative that you can change with ease.

1. Buy a flat bedsheet that matches your bedding. (A sheet is preferable to fabric because most of the measuring and hemming is done for you.)

2. Measure from the top of your box spring to the floor and the length of the bed. (If you want to add a box pleat for a tailored look, add 8 inches to the length measurement.) Then measure the width of the bed plus 4 inches. The skirt will wrap around the end of the bed and the side panels will cover those edges.

3. Cut the side panels from each edge of the sheet (bottom hem). Cut the section for the end of the bed from the remaining portion.

4. Use iron-on fusible tape to hem raw edges.

5. To make the box pleat, find the center of the width of the panel and mark it with some chalk. Measure out 4 inches on both sides of that point, marking the ends. Fold the end marks into the center so you have a 2-inch pleat on either side. Secure it with iron-on fusible tape.

6. Use hook-and-loop tape to adhere the panels directly to the box spring.

A B C D E F G H I J K L M N O P Q R S T U V W X Y Z

GARAGE
STORAGE

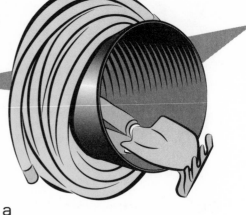

Look between the lines to find extra storage space in your garage. There is a lot of unused storage space between the unfinished wall studs!

➤ Cut pieces of 2x4 to size and secure between the studs. These great custom shelves can be used to hold everything from painting supplies to gardening equipment.

➤ Drill some holes through a couple of shelves and create a handy spot to put tools. Attach a few large screw eyes to the front of a shelf to give you a spot for your screwdrivers.

➤ This space between the studs can also be used to store rakes and shovels. Attach a couple of large screw eyes to two studs and string a bungee cord across the eyes. Slip the tools behind the cord.

➤ For yard tools that are too big to fit between the studs, add a tool rack or a shaker peg rack to the wall. You can also use the rack to store sports equipment.

➤ Keep the hose from sitting in a heap on the floor by attaching a metal bucket securely to the wall. You can put your garden hose around the bucket and your attachments or garden tools inside.

HALLOWEEN PUMPKIN POINTERS

Trick or treat! The trick is to follow
a few simple ideas. The treat?
A frightfully perfect pumpkin every time.

1. Put down several layers of newspaper to protect
your work surface. A table is a great choice because
it's easier to scoop from above the pumpkin. You
should also draw some practice faces on paper.

2. A drywall saw is a great tool for making the rough
cuts—like around the stem. Its pointed tip and
heavy-duty teeth cut easily through that tough
pumpkin shell. Then, use an ice cream scoop to clean
out the guts; it's designed to scoop through hard
substances! A melon baller can help you with the
final detailing inside.

3. Transfer your face design to the pumpkin with a
permanent marker, then start carving. A pointed
serrated knife will make short work of cutting.

4. After you've finished carving the pumpkin,
smear a thin coat of petroleum jelly over the
exposed pumpkin flesh to help preserve it.

> **TIP:** *Be careful when using
> knives, saws, and candles.*

Mrs. Fixit's
AMAZING!

Put a birthday candle
in the jar of petroleum
jelly and stick it in the
pumpkin. The candle will
burn safely for hours
without tipping over.

Safety Tip

A B C D E F G H I J K L M N O P Q R S T U V W X Y Z

HALLOWEEN SAFETY

Ghosts, goblins, and ghouls are all part of the fun of Halloween, but safety should be a priority. Here are some tips to make Halloween scary but safe.

➤ Jack-o'-lanterns are a holiday favorite, but they can be dangerous if candles tip over. Put a votive candle inside an empty tuna can inside your pumpkin. The sides of the can are low, so the candle's light will radiate out of the top. If the candle tips, it will fall into the can, not into the pumpkin.

> **TIP:** *Don't put the jack-o'-lantern near curtains or in a high traffic area where it can be knocked over easily.*

➤ Don't want to use a candle? Use a short string of Christmas lights. Lay them on some foil in the bottom of the pumpkin, thread them through a hole in the back, and plug into a nearby outlet.

➤ To keep little ones safe while they're trick-or-treating, attach reflective tape to the back of their costumes, their shoes, and their treat bags.

➤ Grab an iridescent gift bag for the kids' treats. The metallic prisms are reflective in the dark! You could also paint an old bucket with glow-in-the-dark paint.

HOME OFFICE HINTS

Setting up a home office can be a chore, but I have some ideas to get you set up, organized, and ready to go!

➤ When you're setting up your computer, the tangled mess of wires under your desk can make you crazy. As you install the computer, take a minute to label all of the wires. Use hang tags on a string, silver key tags, or a specialized computer-labeling system from the home-office supply store to designate the printer, the monitor, the keyboard, and whatever else is under there!

> **TIP:** *It's also a good idea to label all the wires to your entertainment systems. If you have a problem with any element, you will be able to locate the wire you need quickly and easily.*

➤ Corral the wires together so they have a neater appearance and they don't accidentally get yanked out of the machine. There are some cool wire-coralling tubes you can buy for the purpose, but it's just as easy to use a length of PVC pipe, pipe insulation—or simple cardboard tubes—to hold the wires in place.

➤ Start with an organized desktop: For an inexpensive organization system, pick up unused paint cans at your local paint store or home center. Use the quart-size cans for pencils, pens, scissors, and markers. Use gallon cans to organize mail and other papers. You can line up several on a shelf or attach them to the wall.

➤ For more comfortable, homelike feel use photo boxes for attractive storage.

ABCDEFG**H**IJKLMNOPQRSTUVWXYZ

KID CALAMITIES

Life with kids is never dull or calm.
I have a few tips to help you out.

➤ If you've ever given your child medicine only to have it spit back out, try treating your little one with a frozen pop stick before the medicine. The cold will numb his or her tongue so he or she won't taste the bitter medicine.

➤ For a child sick in bed, use a 9x12 aluminum or stainless-steel baking dish as a bed tray; this catches little spills before they end up on the blankets.

➤ Keep mismatched socks around; they're the perfect size for a couple of pieces of ice to soothe a boo-boo.

➤ Also, slip a sock over a bar of soap for an easy nonslip grip in the tub.

➤ If your child doesn't like having his or her hair rinsed in the bathtub, use a turkey baster. You'll get a gentle, controlled stream of water to do the job—and the kids will think it's fun to squirt the baster when you're finished.

➤ Keep dolls clean with a nonlotioned baby wipe or a little rubbing alcohol. Simply swab it on the doll's face to remove dirt, ink, and crayon marks.

KITCHEN GARDENING

Look around the kitchen—you may find the perfect plant-care products and fertilizers for your garden or houseplants.

➤ If your azaleas need some help, mix 2 tablespoons of white vinegar into 1 quart of water. Pour at the base of the plant. Azaleas love the acid from the vinegar.

➤ Vinegar is also full of minerals that can enrich the soil for your houseplants. Mix 1 tablespoon of vinegar into 1 gallon of water, and water your plants with the solution.

> TIP: *A little vinegar goes a long way; use the solution on your plants only once every couple weeks.*

➤ Another great fertilizer in your kitchen: Coffee. Work used coffee grounds into the soil around plants. Or dilute 1 cup of coffee with 4 cups of water and use it to water your plants. No coffee? You can use tea or tea bags as well.

➤ Save your eggshells too. Crush them up and sprinkle them around your plants. The shells will decompose slowly and add nutrients to the soil, plus they repel slugs and snails.

➤ Sprinkle some cinnamon around the base of your peony plants to help prevent fungus growth.

➤ To clean up after working in the garden, wet your hands and add a sprinkling of sugar. Then wash with soap and water. The sugar acts as a gentle abrasive to scrub your hands clean.

KITCHEN
KWICKIES

Quick tips that make life a little easier are always welcome in my house; here are some that I'm sure you can use.

➤ Prevent a rusty ring from forming under the coffee can on your cabinet shelves: Simply place the plastic lid from the old can under the new can; it's the perfect coaster to protect your cupboards.

➤ Once the coffee is brewed, put the grounds to work controlling odors in the fridge. Put the grounds in an old plastic container and poke some holes in the container lid. Place the container in the fridge.

➤ Plain kitty litter also works wonders in the kitchen. Sprinkle some kitty litter in the bottom of your garbage can: It will help absorb odors and will catch drips if the bag leaks so you'll have less mess to clean up.

➤ To get a better grip on a stubborn jar lid, grab your rubber gloves. You'll get a nonslip grip and more turning power.

LUBRICANTS

The old saying goes, the squeaky wheel gets the grease, but what do you do if you have run out of oil?

➤ To oil a squeaky hinge, rub it down with some mineral oil and then open and close the door several times to work it in.

➤ Another hinge home solution: Remove the pins from the hinges one at a time. Rub a pencil lead over the pin, and slip it back into place—squeaks will disappear.

➤ Petroleum jelly makes a great no-drip lubricant. Rub it into an offending squeak and work it back and forth. The squeak will go away in no time.

➤ Loosen up a sticky bike chain by pouring a little vegetable oil on a soft cloth and running the cloth over the entire length of the chain. Or use a spray bottle of vegetable oil to get the oil right where you need it.

> **TIP:** *Don't use vegetable oil as a lubricant on items inside the house; it can turn rancid and smell bad.*

➤ Baby powder is a great all-around lubricant. Sprinkle it on floorboards, stairs, hinges, and wagon wheels.

MAILING MINDERS

'Tis the season to follow these tips to keep your holiday mailing manageable—a little gift from me to you.

➤ Make sure the presents you mail look just as good when they arrive as they did when you wrapped them.

1. Start with the right-size box; don't try cramming a too-big gift into a too-small box.

2. Properly pad the space between the gift and the shipping box. You don't need to spend any money; dry cleaning and grocery bags are great packing materials. Just wad them up as tightly as you can and place several bags inside another bag and wedge your bag buffers around your gift. Other options—egg cartons or even old Easter grass will cushion those packages!

3. To protect the bow, place a deli container, a berry basket, or a ribbon spool over it. There's no way any of those will get crushed.

➤ If you don't have time to sit down and get through your Christmas card list, make it a mobile task. Pack a little bag with a clipboard, a couple of pens, your address book, stamps, and of course, your holiday cards. Bring the bag along to doctor's appointments, the repair shop—anytime you have to sit and wait is an opportune time to work on your holiday cards.

➤ To determine if a letter is too heavy for one first-class stamp, put a paint stick on top of a pencil to create a little see-saw. Place a stack of five quarters toward one end and the letter toward the other, if the quarters stay down, the letter is less than 1 ounce.

MULTIFUNCTION PIECES

Many items in the home can perform tasks they weren't necessarily designed for, so look around and see if you can get some multi-tasking done for yourself.

➤ If you have an old door that you're not using, mount it sideways on the wall above a bed—a great alternative to an expensive headboard.

➤ A plate rack hung in the bathroom can serve as an attractive magazine or towel holder. You could also try using an old toolbox.

➤ Corral necessary clutter—such as phone books, message pads, and remote controls—by stashing them in an attractive basket.

➤ An old picnic basket near the phone holds the phone book and take-out menus, as well as a pen and paper for messages.

➤ Take care of too many remotes by stashing them inside a vintage handbag or a decorative tin—either of which makes a unique decorative accent to your room.

➤ Try a double-duty storage piece: An old piano bench serves as a coffee table, plus magazines and remotes will fit easily inside!

➤ If you use a trunk to store blankets, games, or out-of-season clothes, pull it into the living room and make it serve double-duty as the coffee table.

OTTOMAN
YOU CAN MAKE YOURSELF

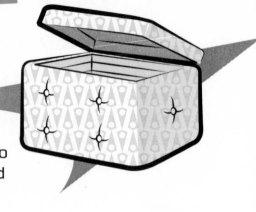

This homemade ottoman does justice to any decorating style—plus it's quick and inexpensive to make.

➤ Start by getting a wooden crate the size you want. If you don't want to build a box, check your local craft store; they're sure to have a good selection.

1. Wrap all sides of the box with regular quilt batting and secure it in place using a staple gun. Cut slits at the corners so you can wrap it snugly without a lot of bulk.

2. Cover the batting with an upholstery fabric that matches your decor. Secure it using the staple gun.

3. Cut a piece of plywood to fit over the opening on top of the box.

4. Cut a piece of 3-inch-thick upholstery foam to the size of the plywood cover, and wrap the foam and plywood together with batting; staple the batting to the plywood.

5. Cover the top with your fabric and staple it in place.

6. Attach the plywood top to the upholstered box using plain hinges on one long side. Now, you have a cute storage ottoman without spending a lot of money.

7. To dress it up, add wooden legs, a dust skirt, or some fringe.

Mrs. Fixit's
AMAZING!

This ottoman also can serve double duty as a filing system. Just add a file rail, found at office supply stores.

Repurposing Tip

OUT OF INGREDIENTS? TRY THESE SUBSTITUTIONS

Next time you're in the middle of a recipe and realize you've run out of a critical ingredient, try one of these in-a-pinch substitutions.

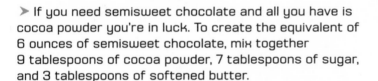

➤ If you need semisweet chocolate and all you have is cocoa powder you're in luck. To create the equivalent of 6 ounces of semisweet chocolate, mix together 9 tablespoons of cocoa powder, 7 tablespoons of sugar, and 3 tablespoons of softened butter.

➤ What do you do if your recipe calls for shortening and you don't have any? Replace it with butter or vice versa—1 cup equals 1 cup in baking.

➤ No buttermilk? No problem! Stir together 1 cup of milk and $1^3/_4$ tablespoons of cream of tartar. Or, add 1 tablespoon of lemon juice to 1 cup of milk.

➤ To create a sour cream substitute, mix 1 cup of milk with 1 tablespoon of white vinegar, and let the mixture sit for 5 minutes before adding it to your recipe.

➤ Use half-and-half in the pumpkin pie if you've run out of evaporated milk.

> **TIP:** *Here is a little advice for your cooking timetable: Don't leave pie making until the end. Everything about pastry needs to be cold—from the ingredients to the room—so if you work on pies first you'll end up with flakier and tastier pies.*

OUT OF THE OFFICE, INTO THE HOUSE

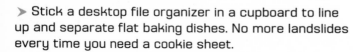

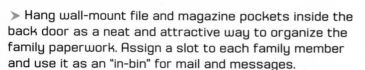

There are lots of office gadgets you can use to help out around the house.

➤ Stick a desktop file organizer in a cupboard to line up and separate flat baking dishes. No more landslides every time you need a cookie sheet.

➤ Hang wall-mount file and magazine pockets inside the back door as a neat and attractive way to organize the family paperwork. Assign a slot to each family member and use it as an "in-bin" for mail and messages.

➤ Hang a desktop blotter calendar in your home as an easy-to-read schedule for the family. Assign each person a different color pen to write down practices, appointments, and play dates so you know where everybody is—and where everybody needs to be.

➤ Binder clips are great for closing up bags in the house; they are less expensive than chip clips and last a lot longer.

PAINT TECHNIQUE TOOLS BEYOND BRUSHES

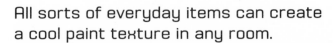

All sorts of everyday items can create a cool paint texture in any room.

> TIP: *As with any painting technique, make sure that you have a good base coat before you get started.*

➤ Plastic Grocery Bags. Pull on a pair of rubber gloves, roll your favorite paint color onto the wall and use a crumpled grocery bag to dab off some of the paint; this technique creates a funky mottled effect.

➤ Old Clothes. Use them the same way you would the plastic grocery bags, but the effect will be softer.

➤ Household Sponges. Dip a dry household sponge into paint, wipe away the excess, and sponge a random pattern onto the wall. For a more interesting look repeat the process with a second complementary color! For a fun effect in a kid's room, cut the sponges into fun shapes, dip them in paint, and "stamp" them in random places around the room.

➤ Potatoes. Cut a large baking potato in half. Draw a simple pattern onto the white of the potato. Use a sharp utility knife to carve the shape. Blot the potato on a paper towel to remove excess moisture. Dip the potato in paint, blot it on a paper towel, and stamp onto the wall. The potato gives you a vintage stencil look.

A B C D E F G H I J K L M N O P Q R S T U V W X Y Z

PEGBOARD STORAGE

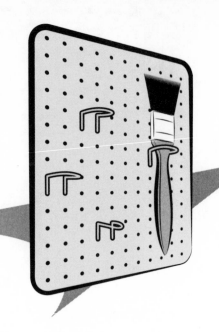

To create easy and inexpensive storage for your basement or garage, use perforated hardboard—or pegboard as it is commonly called. It couldn't be easier to work with.

➤ If you're hanging pegboard on exposed wall studs, simply attach it with some screws.

➤ If you're hanging it on drywall, build a frame around the back to create clearance for storage hooks. Hot glue 1x2 strips to the back of the panel. Place the strips down each side, across the top and bottom and at least one in the center for stability.

TIP: *Have the strips cut to size at the home improvement center and save yourself some prep work.*

1. When the framing is in place, mount the board on the wall. If you're working alone, twist a few drywall screws partway into the studs where you want the bottom of the panel to rest, then set the panel on the screws while you attach it to the wall.

2. Drill pilot holes, drive screws through the panel and the frame directly into the studs, using at least three screws down each side and three down the middle—depending on the size of your panel.

3. Hang the peg hooks on the board, and your items from the pegs—instant organization!

POTTING BENCH

If you've ever priced a potting bench, you know they can be expensive. Save the money by repurposing the old changing table that's gathering dust in the attic.

➤ A changing table is the perfect solution because it is designed to be a good working height, is sturdy (strong enough to hold a squirming baby!), and has lots of storage.

1. If the shelves on the changing table aren't reinforced from below, you may want to add crossbar for stability. Try some L brackets or a couple of sections of 1x2 pine boards.

2. Screw a row of cup hooks onto the side of the table to hold all of your garden tools, keeping them easily in reach.

3. Stock the shelves or drawers with all of your potting supplies.

Mrs. Fixit's AMAZING!

Recycle unused disposable diapers by cutting them into sections and using them to line the bottom of your pots. The diaper squares are absorbent and block soil from leaking out of the pot.

Quick Tip

A B C D E F G H I J K L M N O P Q R S T U V W X Y Z

RECYCLE FOR
CLEANING

There are many past-their-prime household items that can be recycled for cleaning. Here are just a few.

➤ When the bath towels are wearing thin, cut them into equal-sized squares. You can get up to 12 cleaning rags from a single bath towel.

➤ Old socks are perfect for cleaning as is—slip them over your hands and go to work.

➤ Once you've enjoyed your cup of tea, save the tea bag. Allow it to dry and store it with your cleaning supplies. When you're ready to clean, brew up a batch of tea using the bag, and let it cool to room temperature. Tea is great for cleaning woodwork and cabinetry.

➤ Save lemon rinds too. Toss the rinds in the garbage disposal with a couple of ice cubes and grind them up. The combination keeps the blades clean and smelling fresh.

➤ Keep an empty coffee can on top of your dryer, and put used dryer sheets in after every load. Recycle the sheets as wipes to clean electronic equipment and miniblinds.

RECYCLE FOR STORAGE

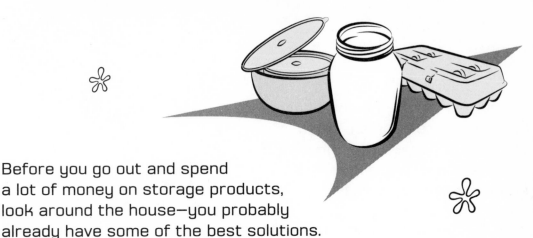

Before you go out and spend
a lot of money on storage products,
look around the house—you probably
already have some of the best solutions.

➤ Those inexpensive food storage containers you picked up for leftovers are perfect for household storage too: They're see-through, they stack, and they come in a variety of shapes and sizes.

➤ Round deli containers have the same superstorage properties. Save them up to have on hand when you need them.

➤ Garbage bags are a great storage container for off-season clothes—and you're sure to always have them on hand. I prefer the clear drawstring type so they don't accidentally get lost. Just fill them up and stow them in a closet until you need the clothes.

➤ Egg cartons have all sorts of compartments. Use them to hold everything from jewelry to craft items—and they stack up in very little space.

➤ An old mayonnaise jar is a perfect hiding place for valuables. Pour some white paint inside and swirl it around to coat the entire surface. Let it dry completely, stash your valuables in it, then put it on a shelf in the cupboard or the back of the refrigerator.

A B C D E F G H I J K L M N O P Q R S T U V W X Y Z

RECYCLE SPORTS EQUIPMENT

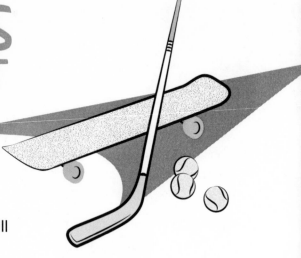

Almost everybody has old, worn, or out-of-date sports equipment stashed at home. Although it may never see another game, it can still serve a purpose.

➤ An old hockey stick is a great tool for dusting hard-to-reach spaces. Pull the leg of an old nylon stocking over it and use it to easily reach under refrigerators and couches, or behind dressers and heavy furniture.

➤ If you have an old golf bag taking up space, use it to tote cleaning supplies around the house: Clip dust cloths to the sides; use the pocket for sprays and polishes. The broom, mop, and hockey stick fit easily inside. String an old swim kickboard or some knee pads to the side to have a cushion for protecting your knees when scrubbing floors.

➤ Create a soft mallet by cutting a slit in a dead tennis ball and slipping it over the head of your hammer.

➤ Slit open four old tennis balls and slip them under the feet of a chair or table you're trying to move for smooth sliding.

➤ Make it easier to scoot along the wall to paint baseboards by sitting on an old skateboard.

➤ Vintage is all the vogue in decorating—old sleds, skis, and other sports equipment make a great addition to a family room or kid's room.

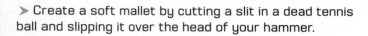

REPURPOSING FURNITURE AND FURNISHINGS

No need to toss old furniture and accessories when you redecorate; here are some great ideas for repurposing what you have.

➤ A table is a table is a table! An old kitchen table can find a new life as a desk in a home office or kid's room.

➤ Cut down the legs of a side table and turn it into a coffee table.

➤ When it's time to discard the dresser, pull out the drawers. Screw casters on each of the bottom four corners of each drawer—these make great underbed storage pieces.

➤ An unused plant stand can be the perfect bedside table, especially in a tiny guest room. You could also use a little chair or kitchen stool as a table in tight spaces.

➤ Or, think in the reverse: A kitchen stool can be reused as a plant stand when you need one.

➤ Extra ceramic tiles from a kitchen or bath redo can be used as trivets. To prevent scratching, back the tiles with felt or cork. Use small tiles as coasters.

➤ Chipped bowls and teacups make perfect planters. Just be sure to put drainage material in the bottom so your plants will thrive.

➤ Think big: Outdated kitchen cabinets make great storage pieces for your basement or garage.

REVAMP IT, REUSE IT, RERUN IT!

Reruns aren't all boring—give some of the items around the house a second life with these clever ideas.

➤ Once a shower curtain is through in the bath, keep it to use as a drop cloth while you're painting, a yard and garden tarp, or even a splat mat under a child's high chair.

➤ Grab an old foam gardening knee pad or swimming kickboard to cushion your knees when you're kneeling by the bathtub to bathe kids or scrub the tub.

➤ Turn old long sleeves from shirts into the perfect plastic bag dispensers. Stuff bags in the top and pull them out one by one from the cuff.

➤ Foam packing peanuts are great drainage for houseplants. Simply place a handful at the bottom of the pot before you fill it with soil.

➤ Old salt and pepper shakers can become your new flour and powdered sugar sprinklers. Simply wash them well and fill one with flour and one with powdered sugar—be sure to label them clearly. Now you have two shakers at the ready when you're baking.

➤ When you get a new refrigerator, keep the ice trays from your old one. Use the trays to freeze extra chicken broth or tomato sauce. When you need some added flavor, just toss a few cubes into your soup or stew.

SCRATCHES ON WOOD FIXED THE NATURAL WAY

If some of the wood furniture in your home is looking a little worn, you'll find some easy and inexpensive fixes right in your kitchen.

➤ To cover scratches on dark wood furniture, make a paste of instant coffee and a few drops of water. Rub the paste into the scratch with a soft cloth, let it sit for a minute, and buff away the excess.

➤ For scratches on lighter wood, rub the meaty part of a walnut into the scratch. It will fill the indentation and blend the scratch with the rest of the wood.

➤ Waxy shoe polish cleans scratches and scuffs from all sorts of wood surfaces. Simply choose the color closest to the wood tone, rub it into the surface, then buff to a shine.

➤ To get rid of white moisture marks on wood, rub the area with a little mineral oil on some superfine steel wool. Make sure you rub very lightly and that you work with the grain of the wood. Or, try white toothpaste; it will get rid of those marks in no time.

➤ If your furniture is looking hazy and dull, mix together 1 cup of room-temperature water and 2 tablespoons of white vinegar. Rub the mixture into the wood and then wipe it off with a clean dry cloth. This will bring back that beautiful finish.

SHORTCUTS FOR THE KITCHEN

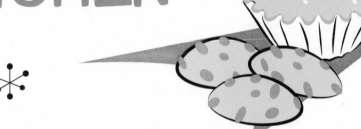

Cooking and baking can cause frustration when you run into problems in the kitchen. These tips will help you get cooking and out of the kitchen faster.

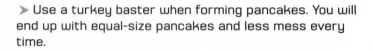

➤ Use a turkey baster when forming pancakes. You will end up with equal-size pancakes and less mess every time.

➤ Use a new powder puff for a nice, even dusting of flour when you're rolling out cookie dough or pastry.

➤ If you're making a cake, use a sprinkle of dry cake mix to coat the pan instead of flour. You won't end up with a white coating on the outside of the cake when it's done.

➤ If your mixing bowls slide across the counter when you run your mixer, put a rubber place mat or rubber jar grip under the bowl before you start. The bowl will stay right where you put it.

➤ If you love to clip recipes from newspapers and magazines, but find that they end up stacked in a kitchen cabinet or drawer, keep an empty photo album in the kitchen. Slip the recipes into the picture slots, and you'll always know where your recipes are when you want them.

SIMPLE PROBLEM SOLVERS

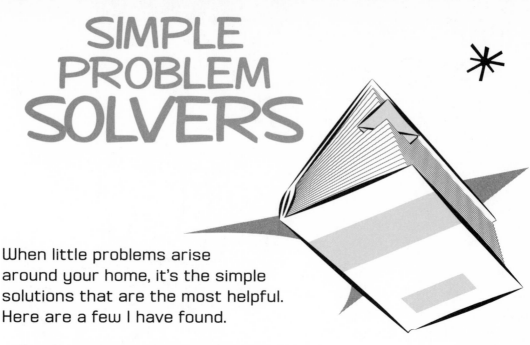

When little problems arise around your home, it's the simple solutions that are the most helpful. Here are a few I have found.

➤ If you're reading a book and need a bookmark that will stay in place, cut a large corner off a junk-mail envelope and slip it over the corner of your page. It will close tight on the page and won't fall out.

➤ To get rid of hair product build up on a curling iron, pour some rubbing alcohol on a terry cloth washcloth and wipe down the curling iron. The alcohol and the texture of the cloth work together to clean away the residue.

➤ When sewing a button in place, put a toothpick between the button and the fabric. This creates just the right amount of space so you don't sew the button on too tight.

> **TIP:** *When sewing on a four-hole button, first sew through two holes and knot the thread; then sew through the other two. This way if the thread unravels from one set of holes, the button will still hold.*

➤ Pilling can make a sweater look old before its time. To get rid of the pilling, shave it off with your electric razor, and your sweater will look new again. The old-fashioned cure for sweater pilling is a sweater stone; you can find them in home solutions stores and mail-order catalogs.

A B C D E F G H I J K L M N O P Q R S T U V W X Y Z

TIME AND MONEY SAVERS FOR HOUSEHOLDS

If you feel like you spend half your time and half your paycheck cleaning the house, I have some time and money-saving tips for you.

➤ Buy commercial cleaners in the big bottle. You'll get twice as much for a lot less money. Simply fill your own inexpensive spray bottles to use the cleaners around the house. Be sure to label the bottles.

➤ If you rarely use a whole steel-wool soap pad when you do the dishes—and it just ends up rusting before you need it again—simply cut it in half and throw it out when you're done. You'll have twice as many, and you won't have to clean up that rusty mess.

➤ Get a beautiful shine the inexpensive way by using a little baby oil instead of furniture polish.

➤ Use an inexpensive car-washing mitt as a dust rag. You'll find you clean much faster, it cleans easily around corners and legs, and you'll use less polish because the mitt will hold it and become a pretreated duster.

➤ Freshen up a dingy toilet by pouring in a scoop of powdered lemonade mix, swishing it around, and letting it sit while you clean the rest of the bathroom. The citric acid leaves a beautiful shine on the bowl.

UNDERSINK CABINET

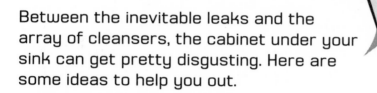

Between the inevitable leaks and the array of cleansers, the cabinet under your sink can get pretty disgusting. Here are some ideas to help you out.

➤ Buy a few individual peel-and-stick vinyl tiles at your home improvement center. (The cost will be next to nothing.) Use them to line the inside of the cabinet. They're sturdier than shelf paper, clean up easily, and protect the bottom and sides of the cabinet from leaks and spills.

➤ A plastic bucket or basin can serve double duty to corral all those cleansers and to serve as the perfect tote when you're doing household chores.

➤ Hang a wire mesh basket on the cabinet door to store your sponges and scrubbers. It keeps the scrubbers handy, and the mesh allows them to dry completely to keep them from getting smelly.

➤ A couple of cup hooks attached to the side of the cabinet hold bottle brushes, feather dusters, and small brooms in place.

➤ To keep the cabinet from smelling musty. Fill a mesh onion bag with chalk or charcoal, and hang it from a cup hook attached to the "roof" of the cabinet. This little sachet will absorb odors and control moisture.

> TIP: *If you have small children in the house, make sure that you install child-safety latches to all cabinets.*

A B C D E F G H I J K L M N O P Q R S T U V W X Y Z

USE IT AGAIN

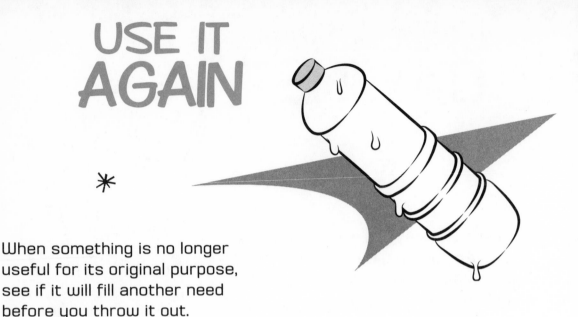

When something is no longer useful for its original purpose, see if it will fill another need before you throw it out.

➤ Old game boards make great lap desks—whether you're paying bills while watching television, or the kids need a surface for coloring during a long car trip.

➤ Refill plastic bottles about three-quarters full with water and store them in your freezer. They make great cold packs for chilling food for picnics and tailgate parties, as well as a contoured ice pack for sore knees or backs.

➤ Put that pile of golf tees to work! Take a scrap of wood and screw small holes about every inch, half near the top of the board, half near the bottom, in a zigzag formation. Tap your golf tees into place and hang the board in the closet for a stylish tie or belt rack.

➤ Keep old candle stubs around for waxing sticking drawers and windows and for lighting fires in the fireplace without scorching your fingers.

➤ Winter tights that have passed their prime are perfect for filling with rice or lentils and putting at the base of a door to stop drafts.

WINDOW TREATMENT ADAPTATIONS

Window treatments don't fit? Whether you've moved, mislaundered, or bought the wrong size, some simple alterations will save you the trouble and cost of replacement.

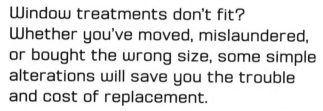

➤ If your curtains fit the window width but are simply too short, secure some ribbon loops across the top of your panels for easy tab tops that will give you just the extra length you need.

➤ If ribbons are too froufrou for your room, pick up some clip-on curtain rings at your local home improvement store. They'll give you that extra bit of length you need and all you do is clip them onto the existing panel—it couldn't be easier!

➤ For really small curtains that don't fit any window, think valance. Depending on the length, you may not even have to alter them. Size them up to the window; if you like the length, just hang them up. If you think they're too long, fold over the top and make a new rod pocket with some thread or fusible tape.

➤ For a temporary change, simply drape the curtain over the rod from the back to the front and add a length of ribbon or trim across the two hems you've just created to add some dimension.

A B C D E F G H I J K L M N O P Q R S T U V W X Y Z

WINDOW TREATMENT ALTERNATIVES

If the price of window treatments has you down, I have some easy and inexpensive alternatives!

> **TIP:** *All of these ideas use a shower tension rod and you may need a sleeve to cover the rod.*

➤ To make a sleeve for your tension rod, cut a piece of fabric at least twice as long as the window, and about 4 inches wide. Fold the fabric in half and use iron-on fusible tape to seal the ends together. Turn the sleeve inside out and slip it over the rod.

➤ For a treatment between cabinets, hang several baskets over the rod, and put it in place. Once it is up, you can add more baskets if you need to. Or for a child's sports-themed room, cover the rod with baseball caps.

➤ Create an easy valance by draping some pretty cloth napkins diagonally over the rod, overlapping them down the rod. Or hang two or three dish towels across a tension rod, one in the center and one at each end. Then hang additional towels at different heights to create a look you want.

➤ For a fun look, forget the tension rod and hang a piece of clothesline across your window and attach dish towels with clip-on clothespins!

➤ If you'd like a decorative topper for some existing curtains, try a square tablecloth. Just drape it diagonally over the curtain. Pin a tassel to the point for a decorative touch.

WINDOW TREATMENTS FOR TOUGH SITUATIONS

Skylights, metal doors, a room with a view—well, let's face it; some windows are just tough to treat. Here are some ideas to help you out.

➤ If you have a steel door, installing curtain rods is a major ordeal. Look for magnetic rods; they hold tight and look great.

➤ To hang a miniblind on a skylight, install a couple of small L brackets on the bottom of window. Slip the bottom ends of the miniblind behind the brackets to hold the blind in place.

➤ For a different look on a skylight, put a cup hook in each of the four corners of the window. Sew drapery rings to the back of a curtain that fits the window. Simply hang up the curtain in place. It's a great look with little effort—and it's as easy to take down as it is to put up.

➤ To dress a window but keep the view, simply wind a strand of silk ivy around the rod. It dresses up the window without blocking the view.

➤ Create privacy for a bathroom window by etching or frosting the glass.

165

WOOD IRONING BOARD INTO A COFFEE TABLE

Whether you see it at a flea market or a yard sale, or you happen to have one in your home, turn that old wooden ironing board into the cutest coffee table.

1. Sand the wood until it is nice and smooth; clean off any dust with a tack cloth.

2. Lower the ironing board to coffee-table height, and add a bolt or a bracket to hold the legs in a stationary position.

3. If your ironing board is the kind that used to fold down out of a cabinet on the wall, you can add prefabricated legs from the local home improvement center. Use brackets to hold the new legs in place. Mark the location for the legs , about 2 inches in from the sides and 6 inches in from the ends (depending, of course, on the size of your board). Screw the brackets into place, and mount the legs to the bracket.

4. Resand the entire piece to get a smooth finish and apply your choice of stain or paint.

WORKSHOP HELPERS

Alternative uses abound all around the house—these ideas will help you in the workshop.

➤ Wooden popsicle sticks are indispensable. I use them to stir or mix small amounts of paint and epoxy, spread putty, and smooth caulk. I also use them to pad the jaws of clamps to protect the surfaces of my projects.

➤ Inexpensive makeup brushes, available at any drugstore, are great for spreading glue, cleaning out small crevices, and adding texture to paint techniques.

➤ Use blocks of green craft foam (they come in packages of 10) on your work surface to hold pencils, utility knives, small tools, and drill bits.

➤ Thoroughly clean out old nail polish bottles and use a medicine dropper to fill them with small amounts of paint. Mark the bottles clearly. You have instant touch-up bottles for any room in the house.

➤ Gutter brackets easily corral extension cords to keep them out of your way.

➤ Muffin tins are the perfect size to hold a variety of small items and keep them organized while you work.

A
B
C
D
E
F
G
H
I
J
K
L
M
N
O
P
Q
R
S
T
U
V
W
X
Y
Z

WORKSHOP TIMESAVERS

A little organization and timesaving know-how will help you get projects done a lot quicker.

➤ Organize your tools into kits rather than one big toolbox—for example, a plumber's kit, a painter's kit, a general repair kit, and a picture-hanging kit.

> TIP: *For exactly what to put in each kit, see the Tool section—starting on p. 170.*

➤ Separate picture hangers into empty film canisters, and label the canisters with the hangers' weights. When you're ready to hang a picture, simply grab the canister you need—no more fishing through a tray of hangers to find the right one.

➤ Mount an old hacksaw blade to the side of the workbench where you're sure you're not going to brush up against it. You can use this as a handy cutter to slice string and cut sandpaper.

➤ In the toolbox, store string spools and sandpaper rolls in an unused waxed paper or plastic wrap box. The spools and rolls stack neatly in the box, and you have a great cutting surface on the side of the box.

➤ Use shower curtain hooks to separate "O" rings, washers, and nuts. Clip the hook onto a belt or toolbox while you're on the job.

➤ A pegboard is indispensable in the workshop, but for items that won't fit on the board, hang a plastic shoe bag across a few pegs. The pockets hold and assortment of items. The items in the bags are easy to see and easy to reach.

WORKSHOP WONDERS

Just like anywhere else in the home, the workshop needs great storage and organization ideas. I've put together some ideas for reusing household items to help you out in the workshop.

➤ Moisture and humidity can seriously cut the life of your sandpaper. Store it in a large plastic ziptop bag to prolong its life. As a bonus, most plastic bags have a space for labeling on the front. Write the grit number right on the bag and find the right paper easily when you need it.

➤ Keep extension cords untangled with an old sock. Cut the toe out of an old sock, then coil the cord. Slip the sock band around the cord to hold it in place.

➤ Snag empty baby food jars for storing small nails and hardware. Maximize storage space by using screws to attach the lids to the underside of a shelf. Screw the jars into their lids for storage.

➤ Another great storage recycling idea from the kitchen is coffee cans. To prevent rust, add 1 tablespoon of baking soda or kitty litter to the bottom of the can.

➤ Check the closet for paintbrush and roller cover storage. Old pants hangers and tie racks provide great storage without taking up much room.

TOOLS

Timid around tools?

I have the must-haves

and how-tos to

get you started!

Remember, you can do it!

"It's just that simple!"

Batteries

It seems like we use more batteries than ever these days. Here are some tips for making them last longer.

➤ Storing batteries in the fridge is an easy way to make them last longer. Stash them in a snack-size zip-top bag; just line them up nice and neat, and seal the top.

➤ To squeeze a little more life out of your batteries scuff the surface of the terminal lightly with an emery board. It will clean off dirt to make a better connection.

➤ Replace all the batteries in an item, rather than just one or two. Leaving the old ones in may seem to stretch the life of the old ones, but it just drains the new ones more quickly.

> **TIP:** *Never dispose of batteries in a fire or they could explode. Check local disposal guidelines.*

➤ The most common, least expensive rechargeable batteries are nickel cadmium. You'll find them in cordless phones, rechargeable toothbrushes, and power razors. The problem with these batteries is what's called the "memory" effect: The batteries "remember" the last charge. If you recharge the battery before they're almost completely drained, you shorten their life. Use nickel cadmium batteries until they're almost out of juice; then recharge them overnight.

➤ If you use battery-powered tools, invest in a second set of batteries so you're not caught in the middle of a project with no power.

EXTENSION CORD SAFETY

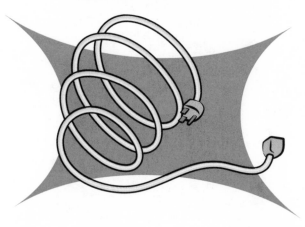

Extension cords are a necessity in any household, but they're not all the same. It's important that you make sure you have the right one for the job to prevent an accident.

➤ Extension cords come in various gauges; it is the gauge that tells how much electricity the cord can handle. The thicker the wire, the lower the gauge, and the more current it can carry.

➤ When using three-prong tools, be sure you use a three-prong cord. Never use an adapter on an extension cord because you're risking serious shock.

➤ If you're working outside, use only cords designated for outdoor use. Every time you use a cord, check the entire length of it for cracks or tears in the housing. If you find a tear or crack, replace the cord.

➤ Another safety measure: Don't run an extension cord from inside to use outside unless it is plugged into a Ground Fault Circuit Interrupter (GFCI) outlet to protect against shock.

➤ If you're using a cord with multiple outlets but you only need one of them, cover the rest with child-safety covers.

➤ If you're looking for a really safe cord, some newer models have GFCIs built right into them. They're worth the investment.

> **TIP:** *It may seem like a no brainer, but it bears repeating: Make sure your tools are turned off before you plug them in!*

TOOL SAFETY TIPS

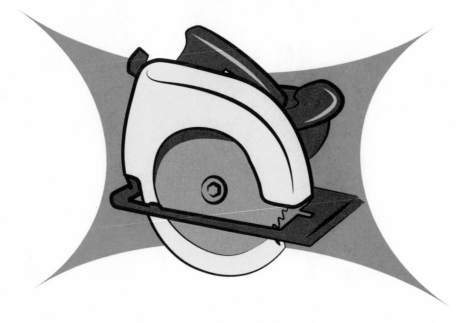

If you have some workshop projects, I have some easy ideas that will help you get through those projects quickly and safely.

➤Whether you're sanding, sawing, or drilling, you'll encounter a lot of dust. Keep yourself safe by wearing some tight-fitting latex gloves for a nonslip grip on those power tools.

➤Also, make sure you wear shoes with rubber soles and good treads for steady footing as the dust piles up.

➤When using a circular saw, make sure you set the blade depth $\frac{1}{4}$-inch deeper than the surface that you're cutting so the saw doesn't jump back at you.

➤Make sure the circular-saw blade has reached full speed before you touch it to the wood. Clear the end of the wood before stopping the blade.

Clamps

Any well-stocked workshop needs clamps, but if you aren't sure exactly what kinds you need, I have some pointers.

➤ Basic C-clamps come in a variety of sizes and can be used on all sorts of projects. Position the clamp over the area to be held in place, and spin the screw end until it is nice and secure on your project. (You may want to use a buffer so you don't mar your project by overtightening. Use pieces of felt, scraps of rubber, or strips of cork.)

➤ Spring-jaw grip clamps also come in a variety of different sizes. They're perfect when you need a clamp in a hurry because you need only one hand free to use them.

➤ Corner clamps are a must if you ever do any mitered projects, such as picture frames. Just insert your corner into the framed area and tighten down all the grips. It holds from all sides with even pressure for nice squared corners.

➤ For bigger projects, you'll need bar clamps. There are several different types; they slide on a bar or pipe. Some tighten down with a screw lever like the C-clamps, but I prefer the trigger-grip variety.

Mrs. Fixit's AMAZING!

For a project where you need to hold two ends together, try a caulking gun. Put a couple of felt buffers in each end and put your repair in there just like you would a caulking tube. Squeeze the trigger until it's nice and tight.

Tool Tip

Cool Tools

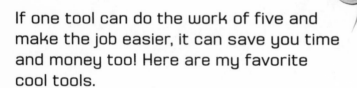

If one tool can do the work of five and make the job easier, it can save you time and money too! Here are my favorite cool tools.

➤ A multipurpose wire tool can help with all your wiring needs. It measures wire, scores, strips, cuts, and crimps and takes up very little room in the toolbox.

➤ Another multifunctional little wonder is a five-in-one painter's tool that works well beyond painting projects. The flat edge opens paint cans, but can also tighten a loose flathead screw. The sharp beveled end will scrape away paint but can also loosen a stuck window. The pointed end will clear out a corner on a window and also strip away caulk. The curved part is great for removing excess paint from a roller! And use the base of the handle to seal a paint can.

➤ An offset screwdriver will save you headaches because its curved end fits easily where other screwdrivers won't.

➤ If you've ever tried to sharpen a carpenter's pencil, you know it can be tough—check out the new square-shank sharpeners made just for carpenter's pencils; they are available at most hardware stores.

Drill Bits

Not exactly sure what drill bit you need for the job? Here's my guide to get you drilling in the right direction.

> **TIP:** *Make sure you wear your safety glasses whenever you're working with tools.*

➤ The most common bit you'll need is a wood-boring twist bit. These bits have a pointed tip and two cutting levels: one cuts the wood, the other lifts the wood chips out of the hole. I recommend buying a set of these bits: They're inexpensive, and you'll have most of the bits you need for home projects.

➤ A spade bit (they resemble a spade with a pointed tip and a wide, flat cutting surface) is used for the same projects as twist bits but when you need a larger hole.

➤ For even larger holes, such as for installing doorknobs or cutting in for pipes, you'll need a hole saw—a round saw with a drill bit protruding from the center to help hold the hole saw steady while drilling.

➤ Another type of bit you may want to have in your toolbox is a masonry bit, also known as a carbide bit. This type of bit is used to drill through brick, concrete, and cinder block.

> **TIP:** *For drilling, always hold your drill perpendicular to the surface you're drilling; you can attach a small level to the top of your drill to help you.*

BASIC TOOL KIT

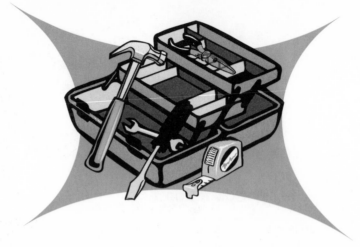

As you empower yourself to become a fixit person, assemble a basic tool kit. Here's the low-down on what you should have. First, buy the best quality tools within your budget. If you buy tools in a kit rather than individually, make sure they're of good quality.

BASIC TOOLS:
- Curved claw hammer—the staple of every toolbox
- Nail set to countersink nails
- Phillips and flathead screwdrivers for all kinds of household repairs from furniture to lighting
- Staple gun for screens, upholstery and a host of other fastening needs
- Power drill for pilot holes in walls and wood

GRIPPING TOOLS:
- Adjustable wrench
- A nut driver is handy to tighten nuts in small spaces
- A pair of needle-nose pliers
- A set of open-end wrenches
- Slip joint pliers

MEASURING TOOLS: These will help you with jobs ranging from hanging shelves and artwork to positioning furniture to checking doors and drawers for square.
- Combination square
- Tape measure
- Torpedo level

CUTTING TOOLS: To cut through more repairs, have these tools on hand.
- Craft and hobby knives
- Hacksaw
- Utility knives
- Wire cutters
- Wood saw

Electrical Gadgets

Installing a GFCI outlet or changing a light switch? I have some indispensable gadgets that you can't do without.

➤ A circuit tester is a simple Y-shaped tool with a light at the bottom of the Y and two leads making the arms of the Y. Use it to verify that the electricity is off when making repairs. First, switch the power off at the circuit box, and then touch the leads to the wires to check for electricity. Check all wire combinations to make sure there is no electricity running through the line before you start working.

➤ A circuit analyzer tests an outlet to be sure it is wired correctly. If it's not, the analyzer will indicate the problem, which, if it's not fixed, could cause serious electrical shock. To use it, plug it in to an outlet. The analyzer will light up at the specific problem. It will detect common improper wiring, such as reversed connections and open wires.

➤ A continuity tester detects whether a circuit is complete. First, make sure the power is off before you use this tool. If you have an extension cord that doesn't seem to be working, no problem: Attach the small alligator clip to the plug's prong and insert the lead into the opposite end. If it lights up, you know the problem is in the outlet or the appliance. You can also use this tool for checking fuses and switches.

Garden Tools

I use my garden tools all the time so I know the value of having them in prime working condition. Here are some tips to keep your garden tools in tip-top shape.

➤ Don't pile tools in the garage or shed. A pile of tools is a safety hazard—they can fall and hurt someone— and the tools will get damaged from impacting with each other. Hang tools so that all sharp edges are protected and secured, so no one gets caught on them.

➤ Clean mud and dirt off your tools after each use to protect from rust. Don't be tempted to scrape the mud off of one tool with another tool or you'll end up dulling them both. Instead, keep a sturdy brush by the door of your garage or shed, brush off the dirt, and put the tools away.

➤ If you're storing tools for an extended period of time, spritz a little penetrating oil or cooking spray on the exposed metal to prevent rusting.

➤ Always check your tools for damage after you use them. Use a sanding sponge to smooth burrs on wooden handles. Tighten or replace loose screws and nuts, and sharpen blades when they get dull.

➤ Small cutting tools, such as pruning shears, can be sharpened by cutting through a piece of fine sandpaper several times. (For tools with larger blades, secure the open blade in a vice and push a file across the factory bevel, working one way in the direction of the bevel.)

180

BEYOND THE BASIC TOOLS

Almost everybody has the basic tools—a hammer, screwdriver, and saw—but there are some tools beyond the basics that you might want to consider adding to your collection.

➤ A combination power drill and screwdriver makes everything from changing cabinet hardware to installing a dead bolt a breeze.

➤ A random orbit sander can help with projects from finish work to stripping paint. It creates a flawless finish, plus these sanders suck dust up through holes in the sandpaper and filter it into a dust bag, leaving less dust than a regular sander.

➤ A circular saw is another tool you may want to invest in. If you do a lot of projects that require a saw, it will save you a lot of time and is more precise than a handsaw.

➤ A multi-position ladder is perfect for a variety of projects: Use it as a regular stepladder, as an extension ladder to reach the roof and clean gutters, or as scaffolding for painting and window washing.

> **TIP:** *Whenever you're working with power tools, wear safety glasses and a safety mask.*

Hammer Helper
NAILING IT DOWN

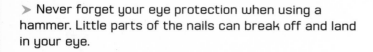

Driving a nail seems like an easy enough task, but there is a right way. In fact, using a hammer the wrong way could lead to accidents and fatigue—here's the right way!

> Never forget your eye protection when using a hammer. Little parts of the nails can break off and land in your eye.

> There are two hammer weights you'll want for household projects. A 16-ounce claw hammer is good for light construction, repair work, and finishing. A larger and stronger 22-ounce hammer will help if you plan to do any framing work. In addition, if you have a small grip, try a 10-ounce hammer.

> The most common mistake people make is holding the hammer too close to the head; they feel like it gives them more control. Instead, hold the hammer near the middle of the handle when you start a nail, and then slide down to the end to drive the nail into place to get maximum driving power.

> To start a large nail, hold the nail shaft between your thumb and forefinger and use your other three fingers to steady your hand. For smaller finish nails and brads, turn your hand palm-side-up and hold the nail between two fingers. This gives you a nice clear view of the nail—and less chance to hit your knuckles.

Mrs. Fixit's AMAZING!

If you're trying to drive a nail into a tight spot and you're having trouble holding it, stick the nail between the teeth of a comb. It will hold it steady so you can tap it into place.

Tool Tip

Hammer Time

I have some easy tips you can use to nail your projects.

➤ If your project requires some serious nailing, use a permanent marker or electrical tape to mark off your hammer handle at 3-, 6-, 9-, and 12-inch increments. Then just hold the hammer handle against the wall and easily eyeball the location for your next nail.

➤ Glue a magnet to the bottom of your hammer. You can stick the handle into the can of nails and collect a few easily.

➤ If you need to remove a nail, crisscross a couple of rubber bands over the top of the hammer. The rubber bands protect the surface while you remove the nail.

➤ If you need more leverage when removing a nail, cut a block of wood into a wedge and put it under the head of your hammer before attempting to pull the nail; it will give you more pulling power. Don't feel like cutting wood? Use a rubber doorstop.

➤ When you're done with your project, clean the head of your hammer with some fine sandpaper to remove wood resins and nail coatings that could cause your hammer to slip the next time you use it.

A B C D E F G H I J K L M N O P Q R S T U V W X Y Z

A
B
C
D
E
F
G
H
I
J
K
L
M
N
O
P
Q
R
S
T
U
V
W
X
Y
Z

Illuminating Ideas

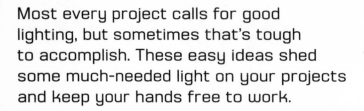

Most every project calls for good lighting, but sometimes that's tough to accomplish. These easy ideas shed some much-needed light on your projects and keep your hands free to work.

➤ It's easy to direct light at your project with either a headlamp or an ear light. Both give off plenty of light for working, and because they move where your head does the light is always aimed right where you need it.

➤ If you've ever tried to prop up a flashlight for some extra illumination you know it can fall and roll away in the middle of a job. You can easily direct that light by making a stand. Put a pair of pliers around the handle of your flashlight and use some rubber bands to hold the handles of the pliers in place. Then prop the light into position.

➤ Get some light into a really tight spot by attaching a night-light to an extension cord and feeding it to the spot you need.

➤ To make sure you have a reliable flashlight at the ready in your toolbox or the car, get the shake variety. They don't need batteries. Simply shake the light back and forth when you're losing power to charge it up.

Mrs. Fixit's
AMAZING!
If you need more light for a project tape a tiny flashlight to the top of your drill for an illuminating helper.

Tool Tip

BASIC LAUNDRY KIT

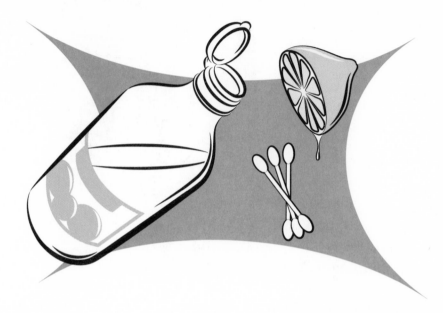

This laundry room toolkit will help you tackle even the toughest of stains.

➤ First tool, good judgment: The easiest way to fight stains is to prevent them, so always check pockets before you do laundry! Pens, crayons, gum, and tissue make a huge mess if you end up washing them by mistake.

➤ White vinegar is a must-have for keeping lint in check; add a cup to the rinse cycle to remove excess lint from your clothing.

➤ Some of the best stain fighters to keep in the laundry room: Hair spray for ink; club soda to keep stains from setting until you can wash them; lemon juice for spots and stains on whites; and unflavored meat tenderizer for protein-based stains such as milk, baby formula, and blood.

➤ Also in the kit:
Plenty of white cloths
Cotton swabs
Soft-bristle toothbrush to gently apply pretreaters to the stains

TIP: A mesh laundry bag for washing delicates keeps them from getting snagged in the washer.

Jigsaws

If you do a lot of projects where you need to cut curves, you need a jigsaw! I have some pointers for choosing the best saw for your needs.

➤ For maximum versatility, choose a variable-speed saw. You can change the speed depending on the type of wood you're cutting and the type of blade you choose.

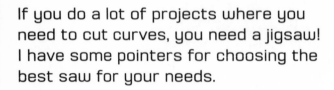

> **TIP:** *When using coarse-tooth blades, use a faster speed. Use a low speed for fine-tooth blades.*

➤ When using a jigsaw, be sure to hold the base plate firmly against your project. This will steady the tool's vibrations and give you a cleaner finish.

➤ Another easy way to ensure a nice finish is to work slowly. If you speed through a job, the saw will bounce and the blade could snap—causing a serious injury.

➤ Unlike other saws, jigsaws cut on the upward stroke, so the top side of your project may splinter. For example, if you're cutting paneling, flip it so the finished side is face-down and any damage will be on the back.

Ladders
HOW TO CHOOSE & USE

Looking for a ladder? Here are some tips for choosing the right ladder for your project—and some ideas for ladder care and storage too!

➤ Whenever you're buying a ladder, look for a seal from either UL (Underwriters Laboratories) or OSHA (Occupational Safety & Health Administration). A seal of approval from either organization ensures the ladder meets safety standards—so you know it is safe.

➤ Take into consideration your weight plus the weight of materials you'll be hauling up the ladder; be sure that the ladder is rated for that weight. You never want to overload a ladder.

➤ For basic household projects and repairs, you will probably want two types of ladder—a step or folding ladder and an extension ladder. These ladders are made in three materials—wood, fiberglass, and aluminum. All three materials will serve you well, but if you're only buying one of each, I suggest fiberglass. It is strong, virtually indestructible, and won't conduct electricity.

Mrs. Fixit's
AMAZING!

Always carry a ladder upright. Grab a rung at about the level your arm hits your leg, and a rung from the other side right up about eye level. Not only is it easier to carry, but you also lower the risk of hurting someone or running into something.

Quick Tip

LADDER SAFETY

Whether you're cleaning your gutters or changing a lightbulb in the ceiling, a ladder is a necessity. But there are a few things you should know so you stay safe and don't accidentally cause damage.

➤ Put socks over the tops of a ladder before you lean it against the house to prevent marring your home's exterior.

➤ When you put a ladder against the house, remember to set it out from the wall a quarter of the height of the ladder. For example, if you have an 8-foot ladder, set it out 2 feet from the house.

➤ Attach a piece of carpet to the bottom rung of a step ladder so you can off wipe your feet before you climb up. This way you won't slip from dirt on your shoes.

➤ When climbing up or down a ladder, always face the ladder. You're much less likely to lose your balance, and you'll have a better hold.

➤ Never step on the top of a ladder. An easy way to remember this is to attach a work apron around the step with a staple gun. You won't climb past the apron, and it's a great place to store your tools, paintbrushes, or anything else you may need up there.

Level It

One of the handiest tools
to have is a level. There are
a few types out there, so I have
a little info to bring you up and on the level.

➤ A carpenter's level has three vials:

1. The center checks for level (horizontal alignment):
Lay it across the top of your project and check
the bubble.

2. The end vial checks for plumb (vertical alignment):
Place it on the side of a project and make sure
it's straight top to bottom.

3. At the other end, there is a diagonal vial that checks
slope at a perfect 45-degree angle. Some
models also have a window on the side so
you can easily take a reading from the floor
(where it could be hard to read otherwise).

➤ A torpedo level is usually about 9 inches long and has
the same vials found on a carpenter's level. Its small
size is key for checking level in hard-to-reach places.

➤ A line level makes it easy to check between two
distant points. It is a couple of inches long and has two
hooks on the back. To use it, run a string taut between
two points. Hook the level over the string and check for
level. You can also slide it back and forth to check
different points along the string.

Levels
BEYOND THE NORM

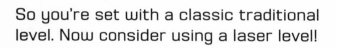

So you're set with a classic traditional level. Now consider using a laser level!

➤ Like any tool, you'll find different grades of laser levels. The basic models attach to your wall with a magnetic hanging pin or drill anchor and use bubble vials like traditional levels to get a straight line. Once your device is level, the tool shoots a laser line out of each side from which you can work.

➤ You can also set these devices on a tabletop, a workbench, or the floor and rotate the level around in its base to project level all the way around the room.

➤ Or you can choose a more sophisticated laser level. These levels attach to the wall the same way as a typical laser level but are self-leveling, so you'll have perfect level every time. Once in place, this level transmits laser lines 10 feet in either direction and has the ability to detect wood, metal, and live wires.

➤ The hands-free feature allows you to move easily on each side of the level. So a project like hanging a whole wall of pictures takes no time at all.

Mrs. Fixit's
AMAZING!
The more sophisticated lasers can also check for plumb (vertical) with a separate beam of light.
Tool Tip

Measuring Must-Haves

From distance to diameter, measuring is an important step in just about every home project. These measuring must-haves will get you ready.

➤ The indispensable tape measure comes in all shapes and sizes. I keep one on each level of the house, one in the car, and one in my bag so I am ready for anything from sizing up a piece of furniture at the flea market to perfect picture placement at home.

➤ A carpenter's rule is another handy-dandy tool. It folds in 6-inch increments and is generally made of wood. This tool makes it easy to measure over your head where a normal tape measure might sag. It also has an extension slide that makes measuring depth and inside areas a snap.

➤ If you measure projects on a regular basis, you need an ultrasonic tape measure, which really isn't a tape at all. Point and click the measure at your start point and then at your end point, and it will calculate the distance instantly. These are perfect for figuring square footage, for calculating projects, and for landscaping.

> TIP: *For more ideas that measure up, see* *Tape Measures That Pack a Punch on p. 209.*

BASIC PAINTER'S KIT

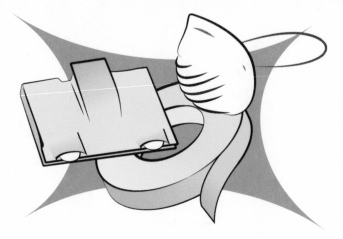

You want to paint a room. You know you need paint, brushes, and rollers, but what else will help your project? I have the perfect painter's toolbox!

START WITH:

➤ Drop cloth for the floor.

➤ Paper edging or painter's masking tape to protect your woodwork. These special types of tape don't stick as much as the regular tapes, so you won't damage the areas you're taping.

Although you can use a trim brush to cut in around corners and woodwork, there are some great tools that will make the job easier.

➤ A wheeled edger will rest on the ceiling or woodwork and make a perfect line every time.

➤ To get into those tight corners, try a pointed roller.

➤ Good lighting is important for a great paint job. Keep a clamp-on light with your painting tools to ensure that you see well while you're working.

➤ A mask—be sure to wear it to protect yourself from the fumes. With lots of choices on the market, choose from simple white masks to a full respirator—all of them work well.

➤ Aluminum foil will line your paint pan and make cleanup easier.

➤ A paper plate under the paint can catches drips.

➤ A roll of string—run a strand across the top of the can and tie it to the handles for dabbing off your brush; the excess drips back in the can.

Painting Pointers

You probably know the basics of painting, but sometimes it's the little things that can make the project go a whole lot smoother. I have some tips to help you out.

➤ Before you tape off an area, rub the stub of an old candle along the edges of both sides of your roll of tape. This will help keep paint from sticking to the tape and pulling off the wall when you remove it!

➤ After taping off an area, run a putty knife along the tape to ensure a tight seal and crisp edges.

➤ When painting a large space, it may be faster and easier to work with a bucket and a roller grid rather than a paint tray—you won't have to stop and refill as often.

➤ A gallon milk jug with the side opposite the handle cut out makes a great "cutting-in tote." Dip the small paint pad inside and scrape the excess off on the cut edge so it drips back into the jug!

> TIP: *When rolling walls, work in a W pattern in small 3-foot sections, evening out the paint as you go.*

➤ If you need to stop in the middle of a job, finish a whole wall and stop at a corner. Otherwise you'll end up with lap marks that will be difficult to mask.

➤ Speaking of stopping in the middle of a job, no need to wash those brushes out just yet. Zip your brushes or rollers into a plastic bag or wrap them in aluminum foil. Then pop them in the freezer. They'll keep until the next day and you'll save yourself some cleanup.

A B C D E F G H I J K L M N O P Q R S T U V W X Y Z

Painting Pointers
CONTINUED

More painting pointers to help you out!

➤ If your room calls for more than a gallon of paint, mix the two cans together. Even though the paint was mixed using the same formula, it can have variations from can to can, and you don't want those variations showing up on your walls!

➤ When cutting in, keep a wet edge to prevent a hatband (that line of paint that looks different than the walls where you cut in). To do this, work in small areas at a time, and roll the walls, blending the paint as you go. Or work with a buddy: One of you can cut in while the other rolls the walls.

➤ I love using a wheeled paint pad for cutting in around a room. Professionals may disagree and opt for a brush, but for the amateur painter, the pad gives nice control, coverage, and crisp, clean edges!

➤ To remove your roller from its handle for cleaning, slip a plastic grocery bag over it, and pull the two apart. Simply drop the roller in your cleaning solution and toss the bag.

➤ To clean the paint out of a paint pad, run it over a wire mesh screen under warm soapy water.

Paint
TOOL PREP

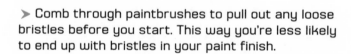

Getting your tools ready for the job
is as important as prepping the room.
These easy ideas will give your work
a picture-perfect finish.

➤ Comb through paintbrushes to pull out any loose
bristles before you start. This way you're less likely
to end up with bristles in your paint finish.

➤ Prevent a fuzzy finish by getting rid of roller lint.
Take some wide masking tape and wrap it around your
roller cover, then pull the tape off, along with all of
the loose fuzzies.

➤ If you hate the paint buildup that gets on the edges
of your roller, prevent the mess by coating the ends
with petroleum jelly before you start. This will also work
on the metal rim around your paintbrushes, or your
hands for that matter.

➤ To prevent having to clean up the roller pan, line the
pan with a disposable liner, aluminum foil, or even a
plastic grocery bag. Then you can just toss the liner
when the job is done—it will save a ton of time.

> TIP: *If your brush has stiff bristles, wash it in*
> *a half gallon of water and a tablespoon*
> *of white vinegar to soften it.*

BASIC CLEANING KIT

Any stain or spill can be tackled, any cleaning dilemma overcome with a basic cleaning kit. Here's what you need.

THE TOOLS:

Remember, quality tools give better results, hands down, so buy the best quality you can afford.

- Broom
- Bucket
- Cloth diapers (For $10 to $15 for a package of 12, you get cleaning cloths that are soft so they won't damage surfaces, white so they won't transfer dyes, and they are wonderfully washable, so they last for years.)
- Dust mop
- Scouring pad with a handle (This type gives you more power.)
- Sponge mop
- Sponges

THE CLEANERS:

- Powdered dishwasher detergent: Yes, it cleans dishes, but it will also cut through stains in your sink and tub and scour soot from brick.
- Rubbing alcohol: It not only disinfects household surfaces but it leaves a streak-free shine on chrome, mirrors, and windows.
- White toothpaste: Gently scours away stains on painted walls and woodwork, white rings on wood furniture, and shines your silver.
- White shaving cream: This is an indispensible spot treater. Use it on carpets, upholstery, clothing, and linens.

Now you're ready for anything!

Sanders with Power

If you do a lot of sanding projects, a power sander is indispensable, but which one is right for your job? I have some tips for making a smart choice.

➤ If refinishing furniture is your game, a detail sander is what you need. It is small enough to fit comfortably in your hand and is designed to sand easily around various nooks and crannies like you find in furniture. These sanders also come with various attachments like a "finger" to help get into the rungs of a chair or the spindles on a staircase.

➤ A variation on the detail sander is the palm sander. Just like the name says, it fits easily into the palm of your hand and is a big help in all sorts of projects. Move these tools with the direction of the grain to keep from scratching the surface.

➤ For projects on which you need a superfine finish, try a random-orbit sander. The sandpaper used with this tool is round. The sander moves in a random circular pattern allowing you to move the sander anywhere on the project without scratching the surface. It also has a dust collection bag to minimize the dust it makes during a project.

➤ Finally, for removing a large amount of material in a short amount of time, try a belt sander. These heavy-duty tools have a belt of sandpaper that wraps around two wheels. When turned on, the belt spins and removes material. These sanders are perfect if you do a lot of rough sanding.

Mrs. Fixit's
AMAZING!

With any sander that you choose, be sure to pick up a good pair of safety glasses and a dust mask to protect yourself.

Safety Tip

Sandpaper

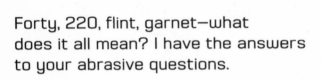

Forty, 220, flint, garnet—what does it all mean? I have the answers to your abrasive questions.

> Sandpaper is made from a variety of materials including flint, emery, garnet, and oxides specialized for projects from removing rust to stripping paint. The most common type of sandpaper is aluminum oxide—the brown paper that you're used to seeing in the hardware store. It's durable and you can use it on surfaces such as metal, fiberglass, and wood.

> Regardless of material, all sandpaper uses the same terminology for the range of grit. The higher the number, the finer the grit; so a 40- or 60-grit sandpaper is good for rough sanding, stripping or shaping, and a 220 grit is used for final buffing.

> Pull a piece of sandpaper back and forth several times over the edge of a workbench, grit side up, before you use it; it makes the paper more flexible which in turn makes it last longer.

> Before you start a project with a sanding block, put a strip of wide tape on the back of your sandpaper. This will give you a cutting guide because it is just the right width and it will keep your paper from ripping on the block so it will last.

Sandpaper
ALTERNATIVES

If you've run out of sandpaper,
or can't use regular sandpaper
in a particular spot, I have some
great alternatives for you to try.

➤ Emery boards are a great substitute; keep a bunch in
your toolbox. They're inexpensive, and have two
different grades of paper on them. Plus, they're small
and stiff, so they reach easily into tight spots that you
otherwise couldn't reach.

➤ For sanding rounded surfaces, try plumber's emery
cloth. This cloth is nice and flexible so you can use an
easy back-and-forth motion to sand the areas. Pick it
up at any hardware or home improvement store.

➤ Check your kitchen sink! Sponges with scrubbers on
the top are a perfect sandpaper alternative. Those with
a white scrubber have about the same abrasion as
600-grit sandpaper. The green scrubbers are
comparable to 220-grit paper. An added bonus: The
sponges are easy to hold onto and they're flexible
enough to get odd-shape areas.

➤ Metal screening fabric—the kind for windows—is a
great alternative to coarse sandpaper for sanding
surfacing compound smooth on drywall. Just wrap the
screening around a small wood block and go to work.

WORKSHOP SAFETY

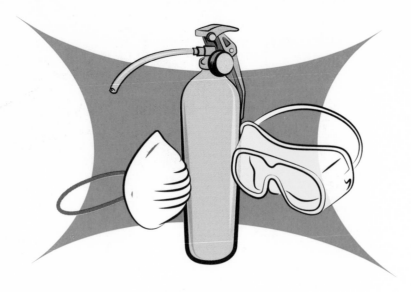

Safety is a secondary concern for some people, but it should be first and foremost, especially in the workshop. I have some pointers to make sure yours is ready.

Protect your eyes, lungs, and ears.

➤ Safety glasses or goggles will shield your eyes from flying debris and dust while you're working on projects.

➤ To protect your lungs from that dust, you can use a simple mask, or buy a respirator, which can protect you from dust and harmful fumes.

➤ If you often use power tools, you'll want a few pairs of earplugs on hand so you don't damage your hearing.

➤ You'll also want to have a box of disposable latex gloves, and a few pairs of heavy-duty stripping gloves on hand to protect your hands from chemicals.

➤ When it comes to safety equipment, you should be ready for anything: Keep a fire extinguisher, a good first-aid kit, and an eye-wash solution on hand.

➤ It's also a good idea to have a telephone in your workshop so if something happens, you'll be able to get to the phone quickly.

"Saw"t- After Tips

Every well-stocked toolbox needs a saw or two. Here are some tips to help you use yours more efficiently and make it last longer!

> **TIP:** *Remember the adage: "Measure twice, cut once!"*

➤ Often when sawing, you can accidentally splinter the wood. Run a length of masking tape along your cut line to keep splintering in check.

➤ When you're using a crosscut handsaw, hold the saw at a 45-degree angle to the wood for a nice smooth cut.

➤ Be sure to saw along the outside of your cut line. It is easy enough to trim away more—but impossible to put it back if you take too much!

➤ For cutting a long piece of wood, put it across a couple of sawhorses and wrap bungee cords or clamps around each sawhorse and the wood to secure it while you work.

➤ When you're done with a project, clean your saw so it doesn't get gummed up. Brush off any sawdust and wipe the blade with a thin layer of lubricating oil.

Mrs. Fixit's
AMAZING!
A quick rule of thumb when choosing a saw, the more teeth per inch, the finer the cut.

Tool Tip

A B C D E F G H I J K L M N O P Q R S T U V W X Y Z

Screwdriver Tips

Screws hold a lot of things together, but sometimes working with them can drive you screwy! Here are some tips to make the job easier.

➤ Screwdrivers aren't one-size-fits-all. Use the right screwdriver for the job or you could risk injury to yourself and damage to the screws.

➤ Keep your screwdriver from slipping by holding the handle perfectly straight and in line with the screw.

➤ For extra assurance, rub the tip of the screwdriver across a piece of chalk before you start. The chalk gives the tip some grip to prevent those slips.

➤ Keep some lip balm with you when you're working with screws. Believe it or not, if you rub the balm over the end of a screw it will make driving it a lot easier.

➤ If you're having trouble holding a screw when starting it, stick the end through a piece of tape and tape it to the screwdriver. This way you'll be able to drive the screw without dropping it, and you can pull the tape off when you're done.

Screws

They keep so many things together, but sometimes trying to work with screws is an exercise in frustration. Here are a few ways to ease the job.

➤ If you have a loose screw that just won't stay in place, try some nail polish. Use the nail polish to paint the screw threads; then put the screw back in place. The nail polish acts like glue and keeps it nice and snug.

➤ An easy way to keep track of screws as you remove them is to grab some masking tape. Unravel a few inches of tape, and when you take out your screws simply stick them to the tape. Now you know exactly where they are when you need to replace them.

➤ Another option for keeping track of screws during a project is using a piece of cardboard. Poke the screws into the corrugated center to hold them in place.

Mrs. Fixit's
AMAZING!

If you spill a bunch of tiny screws (or nails), grab a lid from a plastic container and a heavy-duty magnet. Hold the magnet over the lid, and hold the lid over the nails. The magnet attracts the errant hardware to the lid. Then, hold the lid over the container and release the magnet. Easy pickup!

Tool Tip

A B C D E F G H I J K L M N O P Q R S T U V W X Y Z

BREATHING SAFETY

When you're working on home maintenance projects, protecting yourself is a big concern. One area that you should be sure to focus on is having fresh, safe air to breathe. Keep fumes from building up by always working in a well-ventilated area. Two basic types of safety equipment can also help you breathe easier.

➤ Anytime you're working on a project that stirs up dust, wear a dust mask to protect your lungs. Simple paper-type masks are sold in multipacks at most hardware stores; they are inexpensive and will do the job. I recommend a thick mask that has a replaceable filter in the center near your nose and a metal strip across the top that you can adjust to fit your face.

➤ For big jobs where you may be exposed to toxins (such as asbestos), fumes, or chemicals, use a respirator. These masks come in single- and dual-cartridge styles and are clearly marked on the package as to what type of cartridge offers what type of protection. The cartridges in these masks filter the air and protect your lungs.

TIP: *No matter what type of mask you need, make sure that you clean it when you're finished. Dust masks can be cleaned with a vacuum cleaner; respirators can be wiped down with some rubbing alcohol. Also, replace filters and cartridges often.*

Sharpen It Up

Pencils without points? Dull knives? Shamefully unsharp scissors? I've got the low-down on getting things nice and sharp.

➤ There are hundreds of pencil sharpeners on the market, so why does it seem like you can't find one when you need one. Use a nail file to sharpen your pencil; the rough surface will do a great job. Check your workshop for a wood plane. Just carefully run the pencil over the blade. (This works great on carpenter's pencils, too.)

➤ Dull knives? Check the cupboard: The bottoms of most coffee mugs have an unglazed ring. Just run the blade across the bottom of the mug at an angle and sharpen it like new in a few quick strokes. This also works with a terra-cotta pot, so keep one in the cupboard.

➤ To sharpen those can-opener blades, run a piece of waxed paper through the mechanism. It will clean and sharpen in one quick step.

➤ If dull scissors are a problem, fold a piece of aluminum foil into several thicknesses and snip through it a number of times. You won't believe the difference. Sandpaper will work too. Either method also works great on gardening shears.

A B C D E F G H I J K L M N O P Q R S T U V W X Y Z

Staple Guns

Whether you choose electric or manual, a staple gun will make short work of household jobs from framing to upholstering, so make sure you keep one in your home.

➤ To ensure that your staples end up flush with the surface of your project, make sure that you use the correct size staple for the job. The most common range in size from $\frac{1}{4}$ inch to $\frac{9}{16}$ inch. The smaller versions are for light upholstery and window treatments, and the largest are used for roofing, felt, and insulation board.

➤ A new trend in staplers is the forward-action model. When you use them, you push up toward the top of the device rather than down like the traditional models. This model gives less recoil and will cause less fatigue as you work.

➤ When you're stapling screening or fabric, make sure that you install the staples on an angle to the weave for a stronger hold.

> TIP 1: *Bring the make and model of your stapler with you when buying replacement staples; they are not one-size-fits-all.*
>
> TIP 2: *Remember to always wear eye protection when using staple guns.*

Stick to It

The array of glue on the market today makes choosing the right one a job in itself. I have a handy guide to help you.

➤ The most basic is white glue (the same stuff you used in school). It's great for general indoor use. Try it on small chips in wood, light ceramic repairs, and paper projects. This glue cleans off clothes, carpets, and skin with soap and water.

➤ Next step up—carpenter's glue. It's great for repairs such as wobbly chairs and loose drawer joints.

➤ For faster results on nonporous materials, such as rubber, metal, and plastic, try instant bonding glue. The trick to this glue is to apply it to only one of your broken surfaces, then put the pieces together and hold the repair. It sets up in about 20 seconds. If you're nervous about dripping the glue, buy it in gel form. Clean up is the downside to this one. Use nail polish remover on a cotton swab, but be sure to test for colorfastness on fabric or carpet first.

➤ For the strongest bond, use epoxy. It works inside and out on glass, metal, wood, and plastic. Pull on some gloves and mix the two ingredients that form the epoxy. Apply it immediately; once mixed, epoxy starts to set. Cleanup is tough. While it's still wet, you can use acetone, available at your hardware store.

TIP: *Glue on your fingers? Remove with a little nail polish remover.*

A B C D E F G H I J K L M N O P Q R S T U V W X Y Z

BASIC PLUMBING KIT

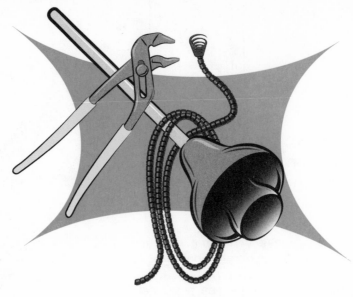

A plumbing emergency kit is a great idea for any household; it will get you through a leaky faucet or a clogged toilet with ease.

> **TIP:** First trick in a plumbing emergency isn't in the toolbox, it's basic knowledge. Know where the shut-offs are for each sink and toilet as well as the whole house.

➤ A good plunger is a must. Make sure it is made of a heavy rubber and has good suction power. Get a bulb-type plunger or one with a fold-out head that sits snugly in the toilet bowl.

➤ A good-quality snake helps free clogs that are deeper in the system.

➤ Assorted pipe wrenches are also a must. The most common needed for household repairs are 10- and 18-inch wrenches.

➤ A big adjustable wrench

➤ A couple of offset screwdrivers will help you get to hard-to-reach places behind sinks and toilets.

SOME TOOLS YOU MIGHT NOT HAVE THOUGHT OF:
➤ Cola—will loosen a sluggish drain or get rid of the rust on a stuck bolt.
➤ Petroleum jelly—will lubricate sticky threads on an aerator or rejuvenate a dried-up valve seat in a toilet.
➤ Magnet on a string—will fish clippers, tweezers, and bobby pins out of a drain.

Tape Measures
THAT PACK A PUNCH

I think everyone has used the classic tape measure—but there are some new types available that really measure up!

➤ The first variation of the traditional tape measure is a voice-recording model that lets you record your measurements. No fumbling for a pencil and paper. Simply take your measurement, press the record button, and read off your measurement. These varieties will hold several measurements and play them back when you need them, saving time and frustration.

➤ Another cool variation on tradition is the battery-powered tape measure—just press a button to extend or retract the tape. This is the perfect tool for getting a measurement in a tight space. So the next time you're stuck under the sink trying to get a clearance measurement you can press a button and take a reading; the tape won't sag or bend like its counterparts. How about woodworking projects? A major frustration is setting the tape measure on one end and walking to the other end of a piece of wood only to have the tape slip off. No more. All you have to do is press the button and hook it over the edge of the wood. The blade is nice and sturdy so it doesn't twist and bend. An ultrasonic or "tapeless measure" is perfect when you're trying to measure a room to estimate wallpaper, paint, or tile. No more climbing up and down ladders or crawling around the floor—the job will be done in no time.

Timesaving Tools

Shortcuts aren't always good, but if they're in the form of a gadget or tool that makes projects easier, I'm all for it. Here are some of my favorite finds.

➤ Patching a wall can be messy: You need surfacing compound, putty knives, and sandpaper. Try a patch stick instead. It twists up, kind of like a stick of deodorant, and you just apply it to the wall. Smooth it out with the straightedge on the cap of the container.

➤ If you've ever spent hours cutting in the edges of your walls before you paint, try a wheeled edger; it cuts prep time to almost nothing. It has little wheels that rest against the ceiling or woodwork, and the paint pad distributes paint evenly along the entire edge.

➤ Copying the contour of moldings and baseboards or installing tile or vinyl flooring around an odd corner is a lot of work, unless you have a contour gauge. Position the tool along the molding you want to copy and press it in. The wires move to copy the exact edge of the molding. Transfer the pattern onto paper, and use it as a template for your project.

Utility Knives

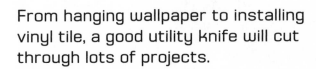

From hanging wallpaper to installing vinyl tile, a good utility knife will cut through lots of projects.

➤ There are two types of utility knives: retractable and fixed blade. In the retractable model, the blade can be moved in and out with the push of a button, and the knife comes apart for blade changes and storage. This knife is a must in every home. You'll use it for everything from cutting wallpaper and drywall to opening packages.

➤ The fixed-blade knives are more professional grade. The blade is stronger, and more durable, and gives you more control when cutting softer materials, such as vinyl tiles and plastics. However, because the blade is fixed, it's not as safe.

➤ Speaking of safety, with either knife, always pull the blade toward you in a slow, controlled motion. Keep your free hand away from the knife. If the blade skips, you can cut yourself. If you're using a straightedge to make your cuts, clamp it down rather than holding it.

➤ Never try to cut through a thick material, such as drywall or foam, with one pass. It will put too much pressure on the blade. Make several passes, fold the material back on itself, then snap it toward you to break.

➤ Change the blades often, especially before starting a big project. The blades are inexpensive, and a sharp blade will get you through a project quickly and safely.

BASIC PICTURE~HANGING KIT

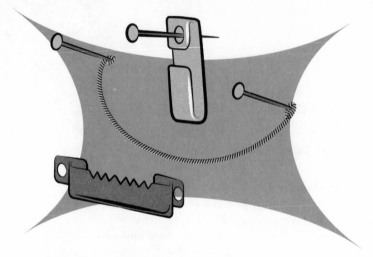

Save time and effort by assembling a picture-hanging kit now. So next time you decide to hang a picture, you know right where everything is.

STOCK THE TOOLBOX WITH:
➤ Chalk
➤ Hammer: just your basic claw hammer will do the trick.
➤ Level
➤ Measuring tape
➤ Picture-hanging wire
➤ Ruler
➤ Sticky notes
➤ Various picture hangers: gummed hangers for very lightweight pictures in plastic frames; hardwall hangers for hanging on cinder block, brick or concrete; traditional hangers and nails, which come in lots of sizes to support different weights; and wall anchors for heavy objects.
➤ Wire cutters

Put everything together in an old tackle box: It's compact, has all sorts of compartments for all of your hangers, and can easily be carried where you need it.

Wall Anchors

Wall anchors are a wall saver when it comes to hanging heavy objects on drywall. I have the lowdown on a variety of these helpful fasteners.

➤ The most common is probably the plastic variety. Drill a pilot hole slightly smaller than the anchor. Then tap the anchor flush into the wall. Twist your screw into the hole in the anchor. As you do, the wings will split apart and press against the wall for a nice strong hold.

➤ An easier option is the self-drilling variety. It looks like a big plastic screw—and works just like one too. Twist in the anchor; then twist in the screw to draw in the anchor.

➤ For a heavier job, use the metal variety. It is used in much the same way. Drill a hole and tap the anchor into place. This type of anchor has teeth that will grip the wall on the outside, so press firmly as you twist your screw into place. As it gets tighter, the wings on the back of the anchor will expand into a star pattern which will give you a nice firm hold on the inside of your wall. This variety also comes in a self-drive model; all you have to do is tap it into place with a hammer. Just tighten the screw until you feel resistance.

Wall Repair and Paint Gadgets

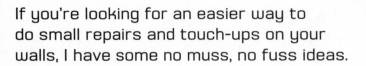

If you're looking for an easier way to do small repairs and touch-ups on your walls, I have some no muss, no fuss ideas.

➤ For a small hole or crack in your wall, use an instant wall-repair patch. To start, be sure the area around the damage is clean and dry. Use a large tablespoon to gently push damaged edges inward. Slowly peel the backing off of the patch and use both hands to position it. Secure the top of the patch to the wall just above the damage. Holding the bottom edges, pull it taut and secure the bottom. Secure the other two sides, but make sure that you don't press hard over the damaged area.

➤ To touch-up paint, try one of the touch-up dispensers at home centers. These look like sneaker polish applicators. Use a funnel to fill the applicator with your wall paint, wet the sponge applicator, and twist it onto the bottle. Squeeze the applicator gently until you see the paint on the sponge, and then just dab it onto the spot for a touch-up.

➤ Another new product: plastic carpet shields, which look like a large window blind slat. Just position the guard on the edge of the carpet and start painting. No need for drop cloths and painter's tape.

Water Savers

Conserving water is good for the environment and saves you money—there are a lot of water-saving devices on the market that can help.

➤ Aerators regulate the water flow coming from sink faucets; the low-flow varieties save water every time you use the faucet. Remove your existing aerator and look for the water flow printed on the side of the unit. Anything above 2.75 gallons per minute is too much. Clean the faucet opening with an old toothbrush and some white vinegar to remove mineral deposits and scale. Then, simply twist a low-flow aerator into place.

➤ Another easy water saver is a replacement showerhead. Did you know that a 10-minute shower can use 50 gallons of water? A low-flow showerhead can reduce that by half. I know, everyone likes a nice strong shower spray, but these new heads are made to give a nice water flow using less water. So remove your old head, use a rubber glove to buffer your wrench so you don't scratch the fittings, clean the openings, and put the new showerhead in place.

➤ Another water guzzler is the toilet. Older models use 5 to 7 gallons of water for each flush; new models use only 1.6 gallons. Short of replacing your toilet, you can force it to use less water by putting a soda bottle filled with water into the tank; this way it takes less water to fill and flush the toilet.

> TIP: *These water-saving devices will end up saving you hundreds of gallons—and dollars.*

BASIC CAR KIT

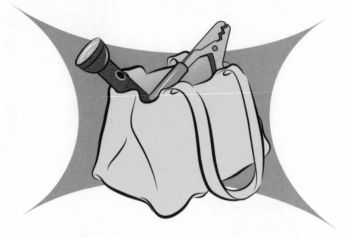

We all make sure our homes are safe and stocked for emergencies, but what about the car?

➤ When you think about your car, you should stock for emergencies, maintenance, and auto paperwork. I suggest a toolbox of sorts for each. My choices: a visor clip CD organizer, travel toiletries case, and a diaper bag.

➤ A diaper bag has many compartments to hold stuff, it's portable and comes with a changing pad you can use to kneel on if you need to change a flat! Stock the diaper bag with a flashlight, batteries, a small tool kit or a good multitool, a tire gauge, jumper cables, extra washer fluid, a blanket, a first-aid kit, and sunscreen. Then stow it in the trunk!

➤ We all need to write down something at one time or another so don't forget paper and pen, or get some that can clip right to your visor.

➤ Use the CD organizer for items you need within reach, a list of emergency numbers and contacts, your registration and insurance cards, and maps.

➤ Use the travel case to corral anything that won't fit into your glove box but that you need in the car; this way they won't fly around if you hit the brakes! Stow the bag in back of the driver's seat so you can always find it!

➤ One last thing: You may want to consider an auto escape hammer with a seatbelt cutter—something you may need that you hope you never have to use.

Wireless Light Controls

From motion detectors to remote switches, wireless light controls can make life a little easier and a whole lot safer.

➤ If you can control the light in your bedroom only by a switch but can never find it in the dark, a remote on/off switch may be just what you're looking for. Plug the lamp into the side of the unit and then plug the receiver into an outlet. Turn the light switch to on. You'll be able to turn the power to the light on and off with the remote control, and you can keep it right next to your bed.

➤ For a ceiling fixture or other light that you have to turn on by a pull chain, try a light-socket-switch kit. Screw the socket receiver into the light fixture and then put the lightbulb in the receiver. Now you can turn on the light with a convenient switch instead of fumbling for a chain.

➤ If you'd like a motion detector for the outside of your home but don't want an entire security system, try a wireless motion detector. Mount the sensor near an entrance or wherever you'd like to detect movement. Plug the lamp into the receiver, and the receiver into the outlet. The sensor will turn on the inside light with any motion, so you'll know when someone is near the house.

Workshop Recycling

Many things in your house can really come in handy in the workshop. Here are a few ideas for repurposing some of them.

➤ Don't throw away a vinyl shower curtain just because the holes have ripped out. It will make a great drop cloth for your next painting project.

➤ Wrap sandpaper around an old deck of cards; the sandpaper will conform to the shape of the deck and give you a good surface for sanding areas such as curved moldings.

➤ You can't have too many coffee cans. You can use them for everything from soaking paintbrushes to organizing nails and screws.

➤ If you're looking for a portable hardware organizer, reuse your old tackle box. All of the little compartments make it easy to sort different sizes of hardware and tools, and it's perfectly portable.

➤ Plastic bottles can be cut up to use as a scoop, a funnel, a handy caddie for dispensing plastic bags, or a string dispenser.

Workshop Storage

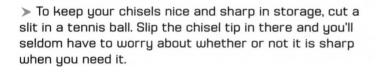

If you're having trouble deciding where and how you should store everything in your workshop, I have just the tips you're looking for.

➤ To keep your chisels nice and sharp in storage, cut a slit in a tennis ball. Slip the chisel tip in there and you'll seldom have to worry about whether or not it is sharp when you need it.

➤ Slip a toilet paper tube over extension cords before you hang them. They won't get tangled up. You can also try ponytail holders with the plastic balls on the end. The plastic balls make it easy to wrap and unwrap the cord.

➤ Slip sandpaper into an accordion file and label the various grits on the tabs. They'll be nice and flat and organized when you need them.

➤ Hang some inexpensive plastic gutter brackets up near the ceiling. It's a great place to store pieces of molding and trim. It will be out of the way, and you won't have to worry about it getting damaged.

➤ Make sure that you hang metal rulers when you put them away to ensure they don't get bent.

Wrenches

Every well-stocked toolbox needs a wrench or two or 10. Anyway, I have the nuts and bolts of this handy tool.

➤ There are a couple of basic styles: adjustable and fixed-head, and there are several fixed-head styles you'll find handy to have.

➤ ADJUSTABLE: Use adjustable wrenches for a variety of household jobs; you can change their size to fit your needs. When using this type, pull on the handle so that the fixed jaw is applying the pressure rather than the weaker adjustable jaw.

➤ FIXED WRENCHES: These squeeze into tighter spaces and are less likely to slip.

➤ Open-ended wrenches are especially useful when you can only access a nut from one side; this wrench's C-shaped head will easily slip into place.

➤ Box wrenches have a closed head to give you more control, but you have to have room to slip the closed wrench over the top of the nut.

➤ Allen wrenches are used to turn headless setscrews, the type often used in unassembled furniture and children's items.

➤ A nut driver works more like a screwdriver than a wrench but has various size sockets at the end to fit over the heads of nuts, bolts, and screws.

➤ And there you have it, the nuts and bolts of wrenches.

Mrs. Fixit's
AMAZING!

If you've ever tried loosening a bolt but ended up stripping it because you turned it in the wrong direction, remember **"righty-tighty, lefty-loosey!"**

Tool Tip

ACKNOWLEDGEMENT

I would like to acknowledge those who helped make this book a reality. First and foremost, my invaluable associate, collaborator and friend Colleen Rosenthal, without whom this book would not have been possible. Her enormous dedication and vision is unwavering. Thank you, is simply not enough for all you do. You are truly a fantastic human being!

Thank you to Al Lauricella for your patience, talent, and humor. You have the eye, and your drumming isn't too bad either! Thanks to my friends at WTVH-5 Syracuse—Loren Tobia, Joe Picciotto, and the rest of the gang who help behind the scenes. Thanks to my fabulous and dedicated team of Jenn Yackle-Kirk, Lucy Cappuccilli-Paris, Amber Wood, and Betsy Cherundolo. Each of your contributions is so vital to the *Mrs. Fixit* brand. Your loyalty and hard work is much appreciated; and I like to think we have a good time too! Lynda, Esther and Karen Jean—thank you for dealing with my crazy schedules and for being there when I need you.

Mark Berryhill—thank you for believing in *Mrs. Fixit* and making the introductions necessary to see this through. I will always be grateful, and I know there's so much more ahead!

Jim Blume, thank you for seeing the vision and making it happen so quickly. It has been such a privilege and a joy working with your incredibly professional staff at Meredith. They are truly terrific! Linda Raglan Cunningham—thank you for assigning such an awesome team to work on my book. Denise Caringer—thank you for your commitment and support. Paula Marshall—it has been a pleasure working with an editor as perceptive as you about the vision for this book. Your constant input and perseverance despite the tough times you went through will always be remembered. Cathy Long—you came into this project midstream and never missed a beat. Your drive and enthusiasm always shines through, and I thank you. To the incredible art team of Matt Strelecki, Matthew Eberhart, and Steve Vandervate—each step of the way you surprised me with your ideas and execution, making the book even better than I imagined. You've made the book look fabulous! Super job!

A thank you to Kevin Robson for his knowledge, followup, and dedication to the project. Thank you Mike Davis for your creativity and artistic flair that makes your work a standout. Thanks to the members of my technical crew, who are always there when I need them: The Abt Boys, Woody, Steve, and Karen. Thanks to my friend, Cheryl, for always being ready to pick up and travel for adventure! And Rita, thank you again for your support and advice.

Of course, heartfelt thanks to my immediate and extended family: My husband Jim for his support and encouragement. I am so grateful for our life together. Pete, or JP, as he likes to be called—I am so lucky to have such a good kid! My parents, Peter and Phyllis. Janet, Jamey, Jack, Lee, Eric, Audrey, Patrick, Pat, Abbey, Jamie, Megan, Chris, Brian, Mike, Tony, Anthony, Peter P., David, Peter C., GG, Richard, William, Dave, Luann, Ben, Colleen and Max, and Jesse!

Finally, a huge thank you to all of you who have watched, listened or e-mailed. I'm so happy that I can share my experiences with you and help empower you to realize that it really is "just that simple!"

Mrs. Fixit

INDEX